SOMEONE
LIKE
ME

SOMEONE LIKE ME

LIKE

ME

HOW ONE UNDOCUMENTED GIRL
FOUGHT FOR HER AMERICAN DREAM

JULISSA ARCE

(L)(B)

LITTLE, BROWN AND COMPANY

Little, Brown and Company
Hachette Book Group
1290 Avenue of the Americas, New York, NY 10104
Visit us at LBYR.com

First Edition: September 2018

Little, Brown and Company is a division of Hachette Book Group, Inc. The Little,
Brown name and logo are trademarks of Hachette Book Group, Inc.

The publisher is not responsible for websites (or their content) that are not owned
by the publisher.

Photographs from insert courtesy of Julissa Arce

Library of Congress Cataloging-in-Publication Data
Names: Arce, Julissa, author.
Title: Someone like me: how one undocumented girl fought for her
American dream / Julissa Arce.
Description: First edition. | New York : Little, Brown and Company, [2018] |
Audience: For ages 10 and up
Identifiers: LCCN 2018007526| ISBN 9780316481748 (hardcover) | ISBN
9780316481731 (ebook) | ISBN 9780316481687 (library edition ebook)
Subjects: LCSH: Arce, Julissa—Juvenile literature. | Mexican American women—
Texas—Biography—Juvenile literature. | Immigrants—Texas—Biography—Juvenile
literature. | Illegal aliens—Texas—Biography—Juvenile literature. | Mexican
Americans—Biography—Juvenile literature. | LCGFT: Autobiographies.
Classification: LCC E184.M5 A74 2018 | DDC 305.48/86872073—dc23
LC record available at https://lccn.loc.gov/2018007526

ISBNs: 978-0-316-48174-8 (hardcover), 978-0-316-48173-1 (ebook)

Printed in the United States of America

LSC-C

10 9 8 7 6 5 4 3 2 1

For all the Dreamers, who dare
to fight for their American Dream

Dear Reader,

An estimated 800,000 young people who were brought to the United States as children have applied for a government program called DACA (Deferred Action for Childhood Arrivals) since it was established in 2012. DACA made it possible for young people to work legally and allowed them to stay in America despite not being US citizens or having valid visas. Like me, they came to the United States through no choice of their own. Some of them made the journey with their parents when they were babies, and others came to be reunited with their parents as young children. Like me, they grew up in America, went to school, and feel American in every way. They are known as Dreamers.

After many years of living in Mexico without my parents, I came to live with them in Texas. While I had no say in coming to America, I thank my parents for bringing me here so that I could have a better life. My story has a happy ending. I am now a United States citizen. I do not have to worry about being separated from my family. Sadly, the 800,000 Dreamers who applied for the DACA program do not know how their stories will end. In September 2017, the DACA program was terminated and suddenly their future became very uncertain. Without DACA, Dreamers cannot work, drive, and in some cases, go to school. Most important, Dreamers are at risk of being deported and separated from their families.

I originally wrote my story as an adult memoir called *My (Underground) American Dream* to shed light on the plight of undocumented people and to put a human face on the issue of immigration—a topic that tends to be very controversial. I also wanted to share my story with young readers because my own journey in America began when I was only eleven years old. Perhaps some of your classmates or their parents are Dreamers too. *Someone Like Me* is a story about strength and never giving up on your dreams even when the odds are stacked against you. It is about believing in yourself and deeply knowing that you are enough and that you belong.

Dreamers have not given up. They have fought for their right to live and thrive in the United States by marching to the nation's capital, by organizing phone calls to Congress, and by sharing their amazing and unique stories with the American people. This book is dedicated to them.

My hope is that by reading *Someone Like Me*, you will be empowered to pursue your dreams and that you will know that no matter how difficult things might be, there is always a way. Keep pushing forward and never give up on you.

WITH GRATITUDE,
JULISSA ARCE

PART

MIRACLE

ON THE DAY I TURNED three years old, my mom scrambled to get everything ready so we could go to church for my *presentacion de los tres años*. This is the day children are taken to the church to give thanks for their life and receive God's blessing. I had a lot to be thankful for.

I was born in a bathroom stall, two months before I was supposed to arrive. My uncle Alex had to slide his hands under the bathroom door and hold my head. I almost didn't make it past day one of my life, but I survived. My mom reminded me constantly that I had been so strong. She called me her miracle.

My sister Nay, who is five years older than I am, tells a

different version. She said I looked like a little purple rat, and smelled like a toilet.

My dad had hoped for a boy when my oldest sister Aris was born. He had prayed for a boy when my sister Nay arrived. By the time I came into the world, he was desperate to have a son. None of us would be able to grant my dad his wish, but unlike my sisters, I had ruined his chances of *ever* having a baby boy.

When I was born, I got tangled in the umbilical cord. "We were both very sick, and when we were both healthy again, the doctor told me I wouldn't be able to give you a little brother or sister anymore," my mom would say to me.

My dad said he didn't care. "I was so happy when you finally came home from the hospital after being in an incubator for more than a month." But I wondered if my dad took me to soccer games, bought me toy cars, and dressed me in overalls because he *did* wish I had been born a boy.

Now Mom grabbed her purse and a big plastic bag filled with pink balloons, and we made the walk from our second-story apartment up the hill, through the winding cobblestone streets of Taxco, to church. Our parish, Santa

Prisca, is a beautiful cathedral made with pink stones on the outside, and gold walls on the inside. My mom was wearing a white jumpsuit and a gold belt, her hair pulled back tightly. My dad wore a guayabera, a casual white linen shirt, that made his dark skin glow.

Aris, my thirteen-year-old sister, held my hand and as we were nearing the church she said, "You will be in kindergarten soon." She meant it as a point of excitement.

But as I walked down the aisle of the church in my floor-length puffy pink satin dress, only one thought occupied my mind: *I am old enough to be left behind with the nanny.*

Every Wednesday, my parents and I left Taxco to travel to the next *feria*, one of the huge festivals that take place all over Mexico, where my parents rented a booth and sold *cantaritos*, beverages served in jars made of adobe. Aris and Nay couldn't come because they went to school, so they stayed home with Cande, our nanny. I had thought that being my mom's miracle made me special and I could always travel with her. But now that I was three years old, I, too, would be left behind to attend school with my sisters while my parents went to work in cities all over Mexico.

When mass was over, I walked down the aisle with a frown on my face. Despite the flowers that decorated the church, the applause from my family, and the *aww*s from everyone seated in the pews, I was scared.

My mom and dad stood next to each other, waiting at the end of the aisle for me. In her heels my mom was much taller than my dad. When I reached them, Mom said, "My little miracle, look how pretty you are."

"Why do you look so serious? Smile," my dad added.

I wanted to smile; I was excited about my dress, the presents, and the cake I had picked out. But I kept thinking of what Aris had told me: *You will be in kindergarten soon.* It wouldn't matter if I was my mom's miracle; I would still be left behind, sometimes for weeks at a time.

My mom and dad walked ahead to get everything ready for the party at my maternal grandmother Mama Silvia's house. All our birthday parties and holidays were held at her house. Even though my sisters went to an expensive Catholic school and I was having a big birthday party, our own apartment was old and too small for a party.

I walked with Cande and tried to catch up with my mom, but my legs couldn't move fast enough. Taxco is in the mountains of the southern state of Guerrero, and the uphill and downhill cobblestone streets did not make it easy to walk fast.

"We are almost there, *nenita*," Cande said, calling me her little girl. I saw the huge red bougainvillea tree that ran up the three stories outside my grandmother's house and knew we were close. It was impossible to miss Mama Silvia's house. In winter or spring, the tree's red color popped brightly against the white house. Her home was my favorite place in Taxco. I especially liked that I could flush her toilet by simply pulling a shiny silver handle, a luxury in a small town like Taxco. The single toilet at my apartment needed a bucket of water thrown into it to flush.

The small black gate at the entrance of her house was open and I ran up the few steps made of tiny stones. When I opened the front door, my mom welcomed me with a set of big balloons. "*¡Feliz cumpleaños, mijita!*" I loved it when my mom called me "my little daughter."

My mom led me to the big living room, which was filled with thirty to forty extended family members, including my many cousins.

A clown with a red nose, huge red lips, and a red suit

was making balloons in the shapes of dogs, flowers, and hearts. Songs by Cepillin, the famous Mexican clown, played in the background. We had a dancing contest and played musical chairs, and for a while I got lost in the celebration. I forgot what turning three years old really meant: Soon my parents would leave me behind.

I heard Uncle Alex, my mom's brother who had saved my life, call out, "Chachis! It's time to cut the cake!" *Chachis* was my nickname growing up, because my youngest cousins couldn't pronounce my middle name, Natzely. I ran over to the dining room to blow out the candles and cut the cake. Everyone sang happy birthday—"*Estas son la mañanitas....*"—while I stood on a chair so I could reach the top of the cake.

"Make a wish, *mijita*," my mom said, smiling.

I blew out the candles and wished I could stay two forever.

But time does not stop, not even for a birthday wish.

LA CENTRO

A FEW MONTHS LATER, ON my first day of kinder-garten, I stood in the shower while Cande poured warm water over me from a big round plastic bucket on the floor. Our showerhead didn't work. My mom was in the kitchen making breakfast for my sisters, who had started school a week earlier.

We attended Centro Cultura Y Accion, or "La Centro" as it was best known. La Centro was a K–12, all-girl Catholic school, except for three years of kindergarten when boys were allowed. It was a school for the wealthy kids in Taxco. *We* were not rich. The rich people in Taxco lived on the quiet outskirts of town, in houses with many rooms and gardens. Our building was next to the town's dumpster. We kept the balcony door in my parents' bedroom closed to avoid the smell of rotten food. Our apartment had running water, something a lot of people in our town didn't have. But if we wanted a hot shower, the water had to be warmed on the stove.

We also weren't poor. From the balcony of our apartment, I could see the poor kids in the street walking around with no shoes, helping their parents sell cilantro, onions, tomatoes, and avocados instead of going to school.

We lived on La Calle Nueva, "the new street," even though it was a really old and run-down street in the middle of all the hustle and bustle of town. Eighteen-wheelers filled the street early in the morning, and dozens of men unloaded the trucks and carried produce, milk, and other goods up the street to the Mercado Tetitlan, the main market in town.

"Ready?" Cande asked when she was done putting the finishing touch on my ponytail—a red ribbon to match my red-checkered uniform.

"No!" I said. "I don't want to go."

"You look so pretty. Your mom is taking you to school. Isn't that exciting?" Cande said, trying to cheer me up.

"But she won't be here when I come back," I said.

From then on, I would stay with Cande, Nay, and Aris each time my parents left to sell *cantaritos* at the *ferias*. Cande had been living with us for as long as I could remember, and even though our matching dark-brown skin made me look more like her daughter, she was not my mother. We had other nannies to help out, but only Cande had stuck around for many years.

My mom and I made our way downhill to my new school, passing the houses and shops that lined the street on both sides. The houses are built right next to one another, sharing walls, and they are all painted white, as is the rule in Taxco.

While I walked with my shoulders shrugged and a frown on my face, my mom's face was radiant with pride.

"You are going to learn so much," she said.

She had been one of those children on the street with no shoes and no education, and now here she was walking me to the best school in town.

When we reached the school entrance, she said, "I

love you, *mija*. I'll be back next Monday." And with that, I walked into La Centro, and she left town with my dad.

The teacher, Maestra Isabel, welcomed us and said, "When I call your name, please introduce yourself."

I was the first one to be called. "Julissa Arce," she said.

"Julissa *La Longanisa*," a boy called out.

"That's not my name!" I yelled.

"Julissa *La Longanisa*," the boy called out again, and all my new classmates laughed and joined the chant. I hated being called a sausage, but even I had to admit, it had a ring to it.

"Stop that!" Maestra Isabel warned.

It didn't help. The chants followed me to the playground that day, and until I started elementary school three years later.

It didn't take long for me to learn why La Centro was the school for the rich kids. The students had parents who owned hotels, buildings, and even silver mines. In order for me to attend this school, my mom and dad traveled all over Mexico, selling *cantaritos*, working fifteen- to eighteen-hour days, standing on their feet all day.

My mom enrolled my sisters and me in etiquette classes so that we knew how to behave at our classmates' fancy parties. We took art, English, piano, dance, and swimming lessons, despite the fact that paying for our school tuition was already a struggle. My parents wanted to give my sisters and me all the opportunities they didn't have, and were willing to sacrifice for it.

I wasn't very good at straddling the line between the rich world of my daily life at school and the world I actually lived in. But the kids outside my school didn't know that; they just saw my school uniform as a sign of wealth. One day, when Cande picked me up, there was a group of kids from the public school gathered outside the main entrance of La Centro. Their uniforms were different than ours— that is how we could tell who went to another school.

Cande and I sat on a bench in the courtyard waiting for my sisters so we could all go visit Mama Silvia. When school got out, the kids from the public school started chanting, "Here come the *fresas*."

I saw my sisters and ran to them. "Oh look, a *fresita*," a "little snob," one of the kids said.

Nay yelled back at them, "Leave her alone!"

"Look, the *Hello Kitty* is getting mad," the kids said.

Nay had a round face with chubby cheeks. When she got mad, she did look a little like an angry Hello Kitty.

"*¡Centro Cultura Y Accion es para los que sienten calentura en su calzon!*" the kids kept yelling.

"Why do they think we have a fever in our underwear?" I asked Aris.

She ignored me. "Are you okay, Nay?"

"Yeah, stupid *nacos*," Nay said, using her own insults, calling the kids from public school "tacky."

"Nay, stop it! That's not ladylike," Aris said.

I didn't even like the kids at my school. *They* were snobs, calling me "*longanisa*" every day.

I wanted to yell, "We're not rich like them!" But I didn't say anything; I just held Nay's hand. Just like the street I lived on was called the new street, even though it was far from new, I went to a school for rich kids but I wasn't rich at all. I felt like a fraud who didn't really belong anywhere.

ALL TOGETHER

BY THE TIME I STARTED elementary school when I was six, my parents had begun construction on a house across the street, and the money from each *cantarito* they sold went to pay for our tuition and the material and labor for my mom's dream house. In the meantime, we kept living in our two-bedroom apartment, where none of the rooms had doors.

From the window, as Cande braided my hair each morning, I saw the new house go up brick by brick. "Mama Cande, how many *cantaritos* does Mami have to sell to come back home forever?" I asked Cande one morning.

"I don't know, *nenita*," she said.

After spending most of my days with Cande, I started calling her Mama Cande. I became very attached to her, especially because other nannies had left me for better opportunities in the United States, but Cande had stayed.

Even though I loved Cande, I still wished for my real mom to braid my hair in the living room of our new house, where she would help me do my homework and play with the dolls she bought me.

I was pleasantly surprised one day to see my mom picking me up from school when I thought she was still away at a *feria*.

"Mami!" I said, running to her.

"We're all going to the Ciudad Valles *feria*," Mom said. "So we can spend your birthday together."

My parents had decided to come back to Taxco and take my sisters and me with them to the twenty-fifth anniversary of the Ciudad Valles *feria*, one of the biggest *ferias* they attended each year.

"Is Mama Cande coming too?" I asked as I wrapped my arms around her small waist.

"She is coming too, but she is just Cande. You only have one mom," Mami said, her smile disappearing.

"But I call Mama Silvia 'Mama,' and she is not my mom," I responded.

My mom let out a sigh. "Yes, but Mama Silvia is your grandma. She is your family."

I was confused because Mom had previously said that Cande was like family. She had worked with us for many years, and we were to treat her like family, not like she was the help.

When we got home, Cande had prepared dinner and said, "*Nenita*, are you hungry yet? Let me make you a plate."

My mom interrupted. "No, I'll serve the plates for the girls. Please finish packing their bags."

I later realized that my mom felt like she was losing me to our nanny. I often thought about all the things I wished I could do with my mom. It didn't occur to me that my mom also wished she could take me to school and make me breakfast, but she had to work.

The next day we made the ten-hour drive to Ciudad Valles, in the north of Mexico. My dad had a Ford pickup truck, and he had installed a camper on the back of it. I rode in the front with my mom and dad while my sisters and Cande rode in the camper.

Once we got to Ciudad Valles, we got right to work. The crowds were huge each night, and our *cantaritos* booth had a line that never seemed to end. Everyone wanted the refreshing orange, lime, and grapefruit soda drink. My sisters and I volunteered to help. The more *cantaritos* we sold, the faster the house could be built, and the sooner our parents could stay home.

"I can cut the oranges and limes," Aris said. She was old enough to handle a knife, so Mom agreed.

Nay helped organize the jars out of their sacks and neatly set them up in rows so they were easily accessible. I helped put salt around the rims and dress the *cantaritos* with an orange wedge. My dad served the *cantaritos*, and my mom took care of the money.

During the day when the crowds were smaller, Mom even let me play cashier. We sold each *cantarito* for fifteen pesos. It was a nice easy number. Even if someone bought three *cantaritos* and paid with a one-hundred-peso bill, it was easy to figure out the change. Eventually, I started memorizing how much change to give a customer with different combinations of *cantaritos* bought and the bills used to pay.

By the end of the third night, my feet and hands hurt—

everything hurt. I knew my mom and dad must be even more exhausted, since they had worked another *feria* the week before coming to Taxco to bring us to Ciudad Valles.

Mom could tell I was tired. "Cande, why don't you and the girls head back to the hotel?"

Almost in unison, my sisters and I cried out, "We're not tired!"

We wanted to soak in each second with our mom and dad, no matter how tired we were. Aris and Nay were older and stronger, but my eyes betrayed me, and not even the sounds from the music and the crowd kept me up. I woke up at the hotel. I was lucky to be sleeping in a hotel. When my parents first started working at the *ferias*, they slept on the floor of the booth. Once, a cockroach climbed into my mom's ear and she screamed and ran around shaking her head and waving her hands in the air, asking for help. My dad finally got her calm enough to take her to the hospital, where they removed the nasty pest.

I woke up the next morning and my mom was already awake, counting the money from the previous day.

"Happy birthday, *mijita*," she said when she saw I was awake.

"Thank you, Mami!" I said. "Can we ride the Ferris wheel today?" I asked. She glanced at the pile of cash on the desk and said, "Yes, I think we can do that before the crowd begins."

We had huevos rancheros at the hotel, rode the Ferris wheel, and then we had chocolate cake at the *cantaritos* booth. I blew out the six candles, and then we went back to work.

I put a tip jar at the booth and told each customer, "It's my birthday today!" and they would say, "Happy birthday," and put a couple of pesos in my jar. At the end of the night, I had over one hundred pesos in birthday tips.

"You better share them. We all did work," Nay said.

"But it's my birthday," I complained.

"You can keep my part," Aris said.

My mom and dad were in high spirits when the *feria* ended, and I knew it must be because we sold a lot of *cantaritos*.

For the first time in years, we had all been in the same place. Family vacations were like this for us. We were working, but we were together, and that's all that mattered.

THE OTHER SIDE

OUR KITCHEN SMELLED LIKE PESO bills. When we came back to Taxco, my mom sat at our small dining table in the kitchen counting all the cash from the *feria*. Every few bills, she licked her thumb and kept counting, separating the money into different piles.

"What are the different piles for?" I asked.

"This one is for your tuition," she said, pointing to a medium-sized pile. "That one is for the house," she said, pointing to the biggest pile, "and that one is to pay all the people who worked with us at the *feria,* and for the materials," she said.

Just like that, all the money we made at the *feria* would be gone.

"You helped make this money, *mija*. And when the house is finished, you can feel proud that you helped to build it."

I looked out the balcony off our kitchen at the shell of the new house across the street, wondering again how many more *cantaritos* we needed to sell to finish it. My mom had been thinking the same thing, and a few weeks after the *feria* at Ciudad Valles, she made an announcement during dinner.

"We're going to *los Estados Unidos* for our next *feria*!" she said excitedly.

My parents weren't going to be selling *cantaritos*. They were going sell Taxco's sterling silver, which my mom viewed as an upgrade. My little hometown in Mexico was known worldwide for its beautiful silver jewelry, and my mom had been working for months to get paperwork approved to be able to sell in the United States.

Images of all the nannies I had lost to the United States filled my mind. *El otro lado*, "the place on the other side," took people and never returned them. Once I overheard my mom giving my dad news about one of my previous nannies: "Gertrudis never made it to California; her mom is afraid she died trying to cross into the United States."

People died attempting to cross the border in search of a better life. Many of those who did make it across safely never came back to Mexico, because returning to the United States was dangerous, or because they were able to make a lot more money in America than they could in Mexico.

Most of my thoughts about the United States came from *Dennis the Menace*, an American cartoon dubbed in Spanish under the title *Daniel el Travieso*. Dennis lived with his mom and dad. The neighborhood was clean and orderly, and all the houses looked the same, with white picket fences and a front yard and backyard. In one episode of *Dennis the Menace*, the cranky neighbor's house is taken away on wheels. Houses in America had wheels! In Taxco, the houses were of all shapes and sizes, placed in no particular order. In fact, from the winding highway that leads to Taxco, the houses looked like boxes, one on top of the other.

"Are you coming back?" I asked nervously.

"Don't worry, *mija*," my mom responded while holding my chin up.

That was not the answer I needed to hear. What if *el otro lado* also took my mom and dad and never returned them?

My dad seemed really excited about their trip north. "When I was a little boy, I made my way to Mexico City just to see the planes. There was a pedestrian bridge close to the airport, and I used to stand there and watch the planes fly above my head. I never thought I'd be able to fly *in* one of them. Now your mom and I are getting on a plane to the United States," he said.

Nay and Aris were also excited about the trip. "Will we get to come with you?" Nay asked.

But we couldn't go. We didn't have the paperwork required to cross the border into the United States. My dad also made it clear that this was not a vacation. They were going to be working the whole time.

"Mami, can you bring me back a Walkman?" Aris asked. Electronics like a portable music player were expensive and hard to come by in our small town, but in the United States everything seemed easily available.

I still had a million questions, but I was afraid of not getting the answers I wanted, so I stayed quiet.

The following week, my mom and dad took their first trip to the United States.

"You'll be back in how many days?" I asked before my mom left.

"Ten days," she said.

A week and a half didn't seem so bad. They had left for longer when they went to *ferias* in the north of Mexico. For the next ten days, I went to school, ate dinner at my grandmother's house, and fought with Nay—my usual routine.

On the tenth day, I waited on the small balcony off our kitchen, which faced La Calle Nueva, for our parents to arrive. It was raining that day, and the wet terra-cotta roofs on the white houses of Taxco made the whole town smell like *cantaritos*.

Evening came and my parents never showed up. *What if* el otro lado *keeps my parents forever?* I worried.

Aris finally called Mama Silvia. "My parents aren't back and we haven't heard from them. Have you heard anything?" Aris asked.

I saw Aris's slender face turn white as she said, "Okay, but when? Are they okay?"

When Aris hung up the phone, she told Nay and me

that my mom had called Mama Silvia hours earlier, but in the middle of the chaos, my grandma forgot to call us. She had spent hours working with lawyers and Mexican customs to try to get my mom back home. Her first priority, she said, was to make sure my mom was safe.

My mom was in danger?

Aris tried to explain what my grandmother had told her. Nay and I sat on my parents' bed and listened attentively.

"You know how Mom was so excited about selling the silver in the United States? Well, she took too much merchandise to San Antonio. They didn't sell enough and had a bunch of silver left over."

It was all too complicated for me to understand at the time, but my parents paid taxes to be able to bring sterling silver jewelry from Mexico into the United States. If they wanted to bring the unsold merchandise back to Mexico, they would have to pay taxes again. They learned this information at the airport as they were checking their bags. Paying more fees was not something my parents could afford to do. They had spent a large portion of their savings purchasing the jewelry in the hope of making a big return on their money.

"So when are they coming back?" I asked Aris.

"They don't know. They might have to stay until they sell more of the jewelry," Aris explained.

I kept track of each day that passed. Not knowing when my parents were coming back made my head spin. Each day my parents were in the United States felt like an eternity. "Are they coming back today?" I asked Aris daily.

"Not today, but they will be here soon," she would say. Two weeks went by and I could tell she was getting worried too. She was the oldest, and therefore she had heard the information firsthand, without any sugarcoating.

It's the first time in my life I remember praying. I would kneel next to my bed before going to sleep, put my hands together, and say, "Virgen de Guadalupe, please bring my parents back."

BACK TO BACK

"I HAVE A SURPRISE FOR you," Cande said when she picked me up from school. "Your papi and mami are back!"

I ran as fast as I could, leaving Cande behind. When I reached the top of the stairs leading to our house, I was out of breath, but I cried out, "Mami! Papi! Please never leave me again." My parents had been gone a month.

Mom and Dad were sitting at the kitchen table, and they both got up from their chairs to hug me. Mom lifted my chin and wiped tears from my face. "Don't cry, *mija*. We're here for now."

I felt a big relief that the United States had returned

my parents, but the words *for now* told me they were going to leave me again.

"Come, *mija*. I brought you some presents," my mom said.

We walked through the narrow hallway leading to my sisters' room, and there was a huge suitcase spilling over with clothes, dolls, shoes, and every beautiful thing America had to offer. I even saw the Walkman Aris had asked for.

Cande helped me try on every shirt, dress, and pair of shoes my mom brought me. When I was done trying everything on she organized it in my closet, which was really a string that hung across two walls in my parents' room.

My parents were home for over a month, but I barely spent any time with them. They were busy making big plans for their new business in America. Now that mom had set up several trade shows, she needed a bigger selection of jewelry to sell.

Every silver craftsman in Taxco came to see her in the hope of having their jewelry sold in fancy places like New York City. My mom ran ads on the radio: "Mrs. Luisa Aviles will be seeing new jewelry this Wednesday from 12:00 to 2:00 PM. All those interested should bring samples to the following address...."

It was chaos in our apartment; our kitchen served as mom's office. The appointments always lasted much longer than two hours. A red staircase with a black metal railing led the way to our apartment, and on appointment days the narrow staircase was lined with men and women all competing for my mom's time and money.

I decided my first order of business was to organize the jewelry sellers. I could hear shouts of "I am next" and "No, I was here before you," followed by "I had to go use the bathroom!"

I went out to the small courtyard that separated the staircase and our front door and announced, "Order, please. Stop the shouting or we won't have more appointments today!" I was only six years old, but my voice was much bigger.

I got one of my school notebooks from my backpack and wrote down the numbers one, two, three, four, etc., on a sheet of paper. I drew a line next to each number and then wrote a matching set of numbers at the end of the line to tear off. I went down the line of people, writing down their names and handing each of them a number.

This way, they didn't have to stand in line in any specific order. If they got hungry and had to leave the line, their spot was safe.

When my mom came outside, she asked, "What is going on?" So I explained my new system and she responded, "That is really smart, *mija*."

"I can help you in the United States too," I said.

Mom smiled, patted my head, and went back inside. From then on, if anyone wanted to see my mom, they had to see me first.

Over the next several months, my parents made many trips to the United States, and back to Taxco to buy more silver jewelry. Each time they came back, my mom looked different, taller, and more confident.

"Let me tell you about the malls," she said on one of her trips back to Mexico. "The shopping malls are out of this world. They have every kind of store. You don't even have to go outside to get to the next store. We sell our jewelry to some of the store owners at the malls too. The United States is a wonderful place."

"What's wrong with the stores here? I love Taxco. The United States has nothing on Taxco," I said, feeling defensive about my hometown.

"*No te pongas brava*," my dad said.

But I couldn't help but feel upset. My parents were changing. Each time they came back to Mexico, it felt like a piece of them stayed in America. I didn't like how much they loved a place where my sisters and I didn't live.

"Don't you like the clothes and toys we bring you?" Mom asked.

In Taxco, we had a few shops. But ever since Mom started traveling to the United States, all my clothes and toys came from America: dresses, white shorts, blond dolls, shiny shoes, and a watch that didn't tell the time but held lip gloss that smelled like strawberry.

Then she added, "*Mija*, even bacon tastes better in America."

Bacon? My mom *ate* bacon? She hadn't eaten red meat in over ten years. Now that she lived in America, she ate pork!

"I still don't eat meat, but occasionally I have bacon with my eggs," she added.

Gross. I preferred *huevos a la Mexicana*, with tomatoes, onions, and jalapeños, like the colors of the Mexican flag.

I sat cross-legged on my bed and said to Mom, "I don't

think I would like it in America. . . . Do they even have tortillas?"

She laughed. "San Antonio has more Mexican restaurants than even Taxco does."

America was changing the way my mom dressed, and even what she ate. What else would change? I began to worry that my parents were starting to love America more than they loved me.

CANDE

ONE DAY, CANDE AND I were sitting at the kitchen table. She said she had something to tell me and didn't want me to be upset.

"*Nenita*, I am getting married."

"Yuppie!" I said, jumping out of my chair to give her a hug.

"*Nena*, I'll have to go live with my husband in Iguala."

Iguala was a larger town about thirty minutes south of Taxco. It was in a valley, making the heat during the day unbearable. Iguala had a movie theater and a pet store, which we didn't have in Taxco then. But it wasn't as pretty. It didn't have beautiful streets made of stones, or houses with terra-cotta roofs.

"How will that work? You live here," I said, still not understanding.

"We still have a month together. I'll come visit you, I promise," she said.

I felt like the pink concrete roof over the kitchen had just fallen on my chest. Despite the noise from the bustling street below, my house felt so quiet. My sisters weren't home from school. My mom and dad were out shopping at the market.

I got up from the table without saying anything and went to my bed. I cried quietly until I fell asleep.

When my mom got home, she woke me up. "Are you okay, *mija*?" she said.

"Tell Cande she can't leave me," I said.

"Don't worry, *mija*. We already have someone new to watch over you. You'll meet her next week."

"Don't be so dramatic," Nay said when she got home that night. "She's not your mom."

Nay didn't seem fazed by my parents' trips, or Cande's departure from our lives. I never saw Nay cry when our parents left, or when they took months to come back. She went to school, did her homework, attended her after-school classes, played with her friends, and went to

33

bed happy. Each night when we talked to our parents, I always said, "I miss you so much," but Nay only said, "Good night." I wished I could be tough like her.

Aris didn't care either. She was a teenager and was too excited about her upcoming *quinceañera* to be bothered. They didn't get it. Nay and Aris had each other, but I only had Cande. When neither of them had time for me, it was Cande who played with me and my Barbie dolls. Cande had only gone to elementary school for a couple of years, but she still tried to help with my homework.

The next morning, Cande woke me up. "Let's get ready for school," she said.

I didn't talk much to her or hold her hand on the way to school. I tried to withhold all my affection, as if building a wall around my heart would soften the blow.

The next week, I met the new nanny. She would overlap with Cande for a month, and when Cande left, the new nanny would live with us full-time. Her name was Maria, and she looked very young, like she could be Aris's age. I didn't like her.

"*Mija*, come say good-bye," my mom said on Cande's last day.

I walked to the kitchen and saw Cande standing at

the front door, wearing a skirt and a blouse my mom had brought her from the United States. The clothes made her look like a *doña* despite her belongings being packed in a big cardboard box that had string wrapped around it to make a handle.

Cande knelt down so she could be as tall as me. "*Nenita*, I am going to miss you very much. Remember how much I love you." She kissed my forehead.

I hugged her and said, "Remember to come visit me."

She did come to visit me a few times, but once she started a family, the visits stopped. My mom and dad came and went into and out of my life every few weeks, but Cande had been a consistent figure, watching me grow since I was a baby. Losing her was one of the toughest things I had to go through. I missed Cande for many years to come.

TACOS AL PASTOR

ONE DAY WHEN I WAS seven, and my parents were back from the United States, my dad and I drove to Landa, a small town only fifteen minutes away from Taxco. But even though it was so close, it felt like a different world. Landa is located deeper in the mountains of Guerrero, where the air is colder and the trees are taller, greener, and more abundant. Pine trees line the roads, and in the winter we collected the pinecones to paint into Christmas ornaments.

In addition to the new house my parents were building on La Calle Nueva, my dad also bought a plot of land in Landa. While Mom wanted a big house in the middle of town, my dad wanted a modest house in the middle of nature. The plot of land was a huge flat space surrounded by mountains.

"Our land goes as far as your eyes can see," my dad said, pointing to the bottom of a mountain in the distance. The sun hit his face and he squinted his eyes as he looked around, making his thick eyebrows arch. We walked through the plot and he showed me where the house was going to be built.

"This is where the house will go, surrounded by the trees," he said.

We made an imaginary outline of the kitchen, the living room, and the bedrooms.

"I want my room to be here," I said as I stood inside our make-believe house.

"Why there?" he asked.

"Because it's right next to y'all's room, and I want to be close to you."

My dad hugged me and kissed my forehead, saying he had another surprise for me.

He opened the bed of his Ford pickup truck and pulled a blanket off a bike. "Wow! That's for me," I said.

When I was a toddler I had a pink tricycle, which I

rode inside Mama Silvia's house. But learning how to ride a bike in the hills of Taxco was more than I could handle. Landa had plenty of flat places to learn. I fell more times than I can remember, but before we left that day I could ride a bike, thanks to my dad.

"You must be starving," my dad said as he put my new bike back in the truck.

"Yes! Can we get tacos al pastor?" I asked.

"Tacos al pastor?" he asked, almost laughing. "Tacos al pastor," he repeated in disbelief. My sisters and I weren't allowed to eat pork or beef because my mom said it was unhealthy, but ever since my parents started traveling to the United States, we would eat meat when they were away.

"Yes, mom eats bacon now, so why can't I eat tacos al pastor?" I asked.

"That seems fair. Get in the truck, and I'll take you."

I walked to the passenger seat, dusted the dirt off my legs, and climbed into the truck. He took me to his favorite spot and taught me the proper way to eat a taco.

"You have to add salsa to the top of the taco before you put lime on it," he said, as he squeezed a few lime drops on the taco. "That way, all the flavors come together.

Then you roll the taco nice and tight. Finally, you tilt your head to the side and put the taco in your mouth."

My mouth watered. I loved watching my dad eat; he thoroughly enjoyed his food. I was so happy to spend the entire day with him. I tried not to think about him leaving to *el otro lado* in a few days.

When we got home, Mom asked if I was hungry. "No, thank you, we ate," I said, throwing a wink my dad's way.

"I took her to eat tacos al pastor," my dad said. My eyes grew big. I couldn't believe he told my mom.

"You did what?" Mom yelled, coming over to inspect my arms and legs. She was looking for signs of food poisoning. The first time Aris and Nay ate pork, they got little red dots all over their bodies, as if they had chicken pox. Aris had a scar on her left temple from scratching, but she told Mom she got it from falling in the street. Mom was furious; she wanted to know why I had disobeyed her.

"You eat bacon!" I cried out. "This isn't the first time I ate tacos al pastor, and I am not going to get sick! You are gone all the time. You can't tell me what to do anymore."

My dad let out a gasp. Mom stayed frozen.

The rotating nannies could never discipline me and my sisters. They were often young girls not much older than Aris.

I had always wanted to please my mom, but I was growing up without her, and when she was home she spoiled us with gifts. This was the first time she had tried to discipline me.

Our aunts and uncles tried to look out for us. If I was on the street playing late at night, Tia Rosi would say to me, "What are you doing out so late, go to your house." If Uncle Alex saw me in the afternoon, he'd ask me, "Have you done your homework?" I even got in trouble with Mama Silvia when she heard me say a bad word I learned in school. But at the end of the day, my sisters and I were mostly responsible for one another.

"Go to Mama Silvia's house; your sisters are there having hot chocolate," she said, looking disappointed.

I wanted to spend the rest of the night with my parents. Every minute they were home I wanted to be with them, even if Mom was yelling at me. As I walked to Mama Silvia's house, I tried to think back to the last time I ate something my mom cooked, but I couldn't remember. I couldn't even remember the last time my parents were home for longer than a week. In the excitement of spending the afternoon with my dad, I hadn't stopped to think that if they bought another plot of land, they would have to spend more time away from us.

AMERICA!

"You, Aris, and Nay are coming to spend this summer with us," Mami said over the phone. My parents had been traveling to the United States for four years, and for the first time, we would be making the trip too.

"I am going to San Antonio with you?" I asked in disbelief. My sisters gathered around and tried to take the phone from me.

"Mami, we're going to Texas?" Nay tried to yell over me.

I was so excited I jumped on the bed. I couldn't sleep all night, thinking of spending the entire summer with my parents.

A month before my mom announced we were going to America, she had missed the Mother's Day festival at my school. I had spent months sewing a place mat to gift her. I sat at the edge of a long table during lunch, watching each of my classmates give their moms gifts. I could not wait for the day to end so I could go home and throw the place mat in the trash. I grabbed my new Barbie backpack that Mom had bought me on her last trip and stuffed the place mat into it. As I was getting ready to leave, Lupe, one of my classmates, yelled out, "There goes the little orphan!"

When Nay got home from school later that day, I was lying down on my bed, watching TV and doing homework.

"Nay, are we orphans? Lupe at school said I was an orphan," I asked, closing my book.

"Of course not. We have parents, and aunts and uncles who love us. We have Mama Silvia, and we have each other," she said, then she hugged me tightly.

The day after Mom told us we'd be traveling with her, I announced to every mean girl in school, "I am going to the United States this summer to visit my parents!" I couldn't believe it! I was going to America!

The girls at school didn't believe me either. "*Se volvio loca*," I heard them murmur. I wasn't going crazy.

"They are just jealous," Nay said when I told her about their comments.

I wasn't an orphan, and soon I would get to see America with my sisters.

On their next trip to Taxco, my parents took my sisters and me to Mexico City to get our passports and tourist visas. In order to travel to the United States as tourists, my parents had to show that they had enough money and property in Mexico. It was not easy to be a tourist in America, but since my parents were doing well financially at the time, we had no problem getting our paperwork quickly.

My eight-year-old heart could not wait. I wanted to zoom from Mexico to the United States in a matter of seconds. Instead, we drove for twenty-four hours from Taxco to Laredo, Texas, in the camper that was attached to my dad's Ford pickup truck.

Once we arrived in Laredo, in the early afternoon, we had to join a long line of people waiting to visit the United States. Since we were tourists, and not US citizens, we couldn't just drive across the bridge that separates

Mexico and the United States without being questioned first. Despite having been thoroughly investigated before we received our visas, we still had to be inspected each time we wanted to go to the United States.

Our camper was checked by immigration officers and their dogs. My mom had all our passports in a plastic bag, and told us to be on our best behavior. We waited in line for over an hour. "This is nothing compared to when we bring new silver jewelry. We have to wait for three or four hours," Mom said.

It was my first glimpse into the journey my parents took every few weeks to be able to provide for us back home. When it was finally our turn, Mom and Dad walked up to the US immigration officer, who sat on a stool behind a tall desk. Mom handed the officer the plastic bag with our passports in it, and the officer looked at the bag and waved for my mom to open it and hand him the passports. Dad stood next to my mom and held Nay's hand. Aris, Nay, and I were smiling and excited about our visit, but the officers' faces looked frozen and incapable of giving a smile.

"What brings you to Laredo?" the officer asked in a

funny-sounding Spanish accent, turning our passports inside out.

"We are here to visit," Mom told the officer.

The officer fired off half a dozen questions: "How long are you coming? Where are you staying? Are you coming to live here? Are you bringing any fruits or vegetables? Any drugs? Are these your kids?"

My mom tried her best to keep up with the questions, but with each one I saw her deflate like a balloon. By the time he was done asking his questions, my palms were sweaty and I felt like a drum was beating inside my chest. We weren't doing anything wrong; we were coming for a vacation in the United States, but the immigration officer made us feel unwelcome before we even stepped foot on American soil.

After we went through customs and had our passports stamped, we got back in the camper and went to McDonald's for Happy Meals. For us, eating McDonald's was a luxury. The closest McDonald's to Taxco was in Mexico City, three hours away. I was fascinated with the box in the shape of a house; I didn't want to throw it away. And I couldn't believe a meal came with a toy. French fries were the most delicious food I'd ever tasted, but the Chicken McNuggets were chewy, and it didn't make sense that they were shaped like bite-sized ovals. I was expecting a thigh or drumstick.

After we ate, we continued to make our way to San Antonio from Laredo on a straight road. There was one more checkpoint, about sixty miles from the Mexico-US border. It was a similar routine as before, with more questions, and dogs and officers inspecting the camper and us. The immigration officer asked us to step outside the vehicle and placed us in a single-file line. I held my mom's hand tightly. A knot formed in my throat and I was sure that if I had to open my mouth to speak no words would come out. He took the passports from my mom and went down the line looking at us and then taking a hard look at each of our passports. I didn't understand why the officers were not friendly. We were just coming to visit America, and yet they were so suspicious of us. When he was done asking questions, I was relieved we could finally make our way to San Antonio.

We got off the I-410 highway on a street called Broadway and drove for a couple of minutes, until we came to a gate. Behind the gate were rows of apartment buildings that all looked the same and were neatly uniformed with gray balconies.

My dad parked the camper, and we made our way to my parents' apartment. The gray door had a sign that read N202. Dad pulled out his keys and opened the door. I ran up the gray-carpeted stairs and began exploring the place where my parents lived.

All these years my parents had traveled back and forth, I had always pictured them in an apartment like the one in Taxco. But this place was nothing like our home.

Their apartment had a big kitchen that looked out to a gray balcony, and there was a dining room table with a glass top and brass chairs.

I made my way to the bedrooms. "Look, Nay! The rooms have doors," I said.

The apartment had two distinct bedrooms that were separated by a hallway, and each room had a white door.

"Dibs on the room in the back," she said.

Aris opened the door to the balcony. "The planes look like they are going to crash into us."

My parents lived close to the airport, and every thirty minutes or so a plane flew right above their apartment.

"Do you like it, *mija*?" my mom asked when I came out of the rooms and back to the living area.

"Yes. It's so big," I said. "The toilets are like Mama Silvia's—they flush with the tiny handle."

"And the showers have hot water too," Dad said.

"You just need a couch," Aris said.

The space that was supposed to be the living room housed tables holding jewelry, packing supplies, and the blue suitcases my parents used to transport the silver jewelry to the trade shows.

We spent a week in San Antonio before embarking on a road trip through the United States. Everything in Texas was bigger. The streets were wide and straight, unlike the small winding streets of Taxco. We ate tacos with tortillas the size of my head. I marveled at the wonders of Sea-World and Six Flags Fiesta Texas in San Antonio.

The rest of our stops coincided with trade shows, where Mom sold Taxco's sterling silver jewelry. We visited the home of Elvis Presley, the American rock-and-roll king, in Memphis, Tennessee. Then we made our way to New Orleans, where I discovered my mom was right about the malls. They were out of this world. We went to a gigantic one that had glass ceilings and indoor trees.

Dad showed us around on most days while Mom worked selling silver jewelry at the trade shows. I wished Mom could spend more time with us, but if she couldn't be a tourist, then I wanted to be her helper.

We made our way from New Orleans to our last stop, in Houston, Texas, where I asked Mom if I could join her at the trade show the next day.

"But your dad is taking you to the zoo tomorrow," she said.

"It's okay. I've been to the zoo in Taxco. I don't care if I miss it," I responded.

The last time I had gone to a zoo, I'd leaned against a cage and a monkey zoomed my way and grabbed my long hair through the bars. Nay and Aris tried to pull me away, but a chunk of my hair had to be cut off because the monkey never let go. So Mom agreed I could join her but warned me it would be hard work.

The trade show was taking place at the Houston convention center. There were rows and rows of vendor booths, selling everything from clothes to sunglasses and jewelry.

My mom's booth was in a corner. We had tables covered in silver jewelry. One table displayed earrings, another rings, and one more bracelets. Mom had a couple of people working with her, Sam and Beverly. Sam was a man she'd met in San Antonio during her first trip to the States. He was balding and wore glasses that made his eyes look really big. Beverly was a very pretty blond woman who was also a teacher who had traveled with my mom during the summer trade shows, but I never saw her again after this trade show.

We could hardly keep up; there were thousands of people at the trade show and they all loved our jewelry. My job was to bag the jewelry once the customer had paid my mom.

"Your customers will love this," my mom would say in her half-broken English. I was impressed that my mom didn't care that her English wasn't perfect. She wasn't worried about being judged, and she wasn't shy. She shined. She was a great salesperson.

I worked extra fast, and tried to be helpful by imitating my mom. If I saw someone trying on a necklace as they decided whether they should buy it for their stores, I would say, "Beautiful—want to see a mirror?" I didn't really know what I was saying, but customers loved it when I said they looked beautiful.

I wanted my mom to see that I could be a big help and that she could bring me with her to the trade shows, like when I was little and she took me to the *ferias*. I wanted to show her that she didn't have to send me back to Mexico when summer was over.

But by lunchtime I was exhausted. My mom made a makeshift mattress from the sheets we used to cover the tables at night so I could take a nap under a table. I could see people's feet peeking through the bottom of the sheets. Even with all the noise, I fell asleep knowing my mom was right there. This was the longest amount of time I had spent with my parents since I was three years old. I didn't want the summer to end.

A few days later, we made the drive back to Mexico from San Antonio. Going through the border to Mexico was a completely different experience. There wasn't a long wait in the "Mexican Citizens" lines, and the Mexican immigration officer greeted us with a smile and a "Welcome back." Even though I knew my parents would go back to America, Mexico felt like my home.

My parents stayed in Taxco for a few weeks to see us start the new school year. My mom took me to school and picked me up on the first day of fourth grade, and then my parents were off to the United States again. It was difficult to see my parents leave, but at least now I knew where they lived and worked. Now, when I imagined their life in America, I could picture the straight American roads they traveled along and hear the planes above my parents' apartment.

A BROKEN WINDOW

AFTER WE CAME BACK FROM our trip to the United States, I didn't see my parents for months. Their phone calls were inconsistent, and we were lucky to hear from them a few times a month. Mama Silvia had told me she was now paying for our tuition.

My parents had been traveling to the United States since I was six. I was now nine years old, and I didn't understand how my parents didn't have money to pay for our tuition after years of working in America.

My parents finally came back to Taxco to sell *cantaritos* during the *Feria de la Plata*. I knew something was wrong. Mama Silvia had also told me she had lent my parents money to work at the *feria*. When I saw my mom the day they arrived, she looked so much older. Her usual upbeat and energetic personality was missing. My dad wasn't making jokes. And there weren't long lines of silver craftsmen waiting to see my mom.

I came home from school one afternoon and found Mom crying at the kitchen table. As soon as she heard me come in, she wiped the tears from her eyes and hugged me.

"Are you okay, Mami?" I asked.

"Everything is going to be okay. Everything is going to be okay," she repeated.

That night I heard raised voices. I got up from my bed and found my parents arguing in the kitchen. Beer cans littered the table. My dad had been drinking.

"No, Papi!" I screamed when I saw him pushing my mom around.

My screaming woke up my sisters. The nanny who slept in a room next to the kitchen didn't wake up, or maybe decided she didn't want to get involved.

"*Mijas*, go back to bed," my mom said through her tears.

"Come on, let's go back to bed," Aris said to Nay. Aris didn't want to be involved either.

Nay noticed our dad was crying. She ran to him and asked him if *he* needed anything.

"No, *mija*. I am sorry I woke you up. Go back to bed." He opened another can of beer.

"We are under a lot of stress, *mija*," my mom said as she walked us down the hallway to our shared room.

A few years later, I found out my parents had lost most of their silver. They had a standard routine of shipping all the sterling silver for their business from Taxco to Nuevo Laredo, Mexico, where they would pick it up, load it into the van, and then drive it through customs at the US border. They had done this dozens of times without incident.

One day, during the trip to San Antonio, they had stopped at a diner on the US side of Laredo. My mom had wanted coffee, or to use the bathroom, or my dad had wanted a sandwich—whatever the reason, they both went inside and left the van for only fifteen minutes. They could see the van from where they were sitting, but those fifteen minutes changed everything. They discovered that one of the windows, which was hidden from their view, had been cut out, and all the silver in the van had been taken.

A short rest stop cost them years of hard work. That

broken window, those fifteen minutes almost destroyed my family.

While we ate breakfast the next morning, my dad apologized to us.

"I am sorry I scared you last night," he said.

"Did you say sorry to Mom?" Aris said with a straight face.

"Yes, I did," he said, looking at my mom, who moved her gaze away from him.

I had never felt this type of tension between my parents before. Their visits were usually full of happiness. They tried to give us all the love they couldn't when they were away.

A couple of days went by and none of us talked about the incident again. Then it was time for the *feria*.

When the two of us were alone I asked my mom, "Mami, is it true that Mama Silvia is paying for my tuition?"

"Ay, my mother! I can't believe she told you that," Mom said, letting out a sigh.

"I haven't seen any men working on the house," I said.

Aris had told me it was because of the rain, but it hadn't rained in a long time.

"Will you ever come back home for good?" I asked when she didn't answer my other questions.

"Don't worry, *mija*. One day, we'll all be together in one place," she said. But one day seemed very far away. A few days after the *feria* was over, my parents went back to the United States for another trade show, and I stayed behind wondering when "one day" would come.

FROM BAD TO WORSE

MY PARENTS WORKED HARD ALL my life, but the year after the silver theft they worked harder than I'd ever seen before. Their trips home were less frequent, and I didn't see my parents for six months. My grandmother had taken over our finances in Mexico. When we needed money for field trips, to buy school supplies, or even to eat tacos al pastor on the weekend, we'd ask Mama Silvia.

When my parents finally came home in the summer, they came bearing terrible news. We were all at Mama Silvia's house when my mom announced she was pregnant. I would no longer be her baby. I stayed quiet, thinking of what I should say. The doctor had told my mom she couldn't have any more kids. *How can this be?* I felt a rush go to my head, and my thoughts were jumbled. "I hate the baby," was what came out of my mouth.

Then the news got worse: The baby was a boy. She tried to tell me it was a miracle. "Your dad and I have prayed for a baby boy for twenty years. God has finally heard our prayers."

I liked how happy she was, especially after seeing her so sad and worried on her last trip to Taxco. But I couldn't wrap my mind around sharing her with another baby.

"But I am your miracle! Mami, I am your miracle," I pleaded, putting my hands over my face.

"*Mija*, don't cry. This is good news," she said.

"You'll have someone new to play with. Won't that be nice?" my dad said.

All I could think was, *He'll live with my parents, in the United States, and I'll be left behind forever. My parents won't love me anymore.* Mom had a new, *better* miracle.

Nay wasn't jealous like me. "A little brother! I knew it would work," she said, running to hug my mom.

Nay told Mom that during a school field trip to Teotihuacan, an ancient city of Mexico, she climbed the

Pyramid of the Sun, the third-largest pyramid in the world, and wished for a little brother.

"How could you do that to me!" I yelled. I never knew Nay wanted a little brother.

My cousin Jessi teased me. *"Te van a bajar del burro."*

I would no longer be the favorite child who sat on the donkey, just like the Virgin Mary did while Joseph walked through the desert to Bethlehem. I was getting kicked off the donkey. I was no longer my mom's miracle baby, and my dad would have the boy he'd always wanted, to dress in overalls and to teach things.

A week after I heard the devastating news that I was going to have a little brother, my mom delivered more bad news. Aris had been accepted to one of the most prestigious colleges in Mexico, two hours away in Cuernavaca. She would be living there when the new school year started.

"It's a great opportunity for Aris. We are very proud of her," my mom said.

I looked nervously at Nay, wondering if she would leave me too.

"Nay is moving with Aris to attend high school."

"You can't do this to me!" I yelled. I had survived years of my parents coming and going, and Cande leaving me to get married, but I didn't know how I was supposed to overcome Nay leaving me too.

Nay hugged me and said, "We will be coming to see you every weekend, I promise."

Aris stayed quiet. I didn't care if she said anything. I wasn't going to miss her. She was hardly around.

Aris was a beautiful girl who got a lot of attention from boys. She had started dating a boy named Victor, and she spent all her time with him. Sometimes she didn't come home until the next morning, to change her uniform and go to school. She'd tell us she went running in the mornings, but we knew better. Nay and I never told our parents, though.

"What will happen to me?" I asked Mom.

"You'll live with Mama Silvia," she answered.

Mama Silvia always looked out for us, and even though she was strict, she really cared about our family. I loved her house. I even liked the thought of living there, instead of at home with a nanny. But I couldn't understand why everyone I loved always left me for better opportunities. My parents would have to work even harder to afford my sisters' tuition. Construction on the house across the street completely stopped, so every penny could go to fund our education. My dad even had to sell his beloved piece of land in Landa to be able to pay the debts they owed after the silver was stolen.

I had an uneasy feeling that the time when we would all live together would never come. Where would we live if they were no longer building our home? A few days later, Mom helped me pack a small suitcase with only a few of my belongings to take to Mama Silvia's. "You don't have to take very much, since on the weekends you'll be back in the apartment with your sisters," she said.

Since I was now living with my grandmother, I wouldn't have a nanny anymore. The day my parents dropped me off, Dad carried my small suitcase and Mom held my hand on the walk to Mama Silvia's house.

I walked into my grandmother's home feeling nervous about what my life would be like living with her, away from my sisters, and with my parents in the United States. It didn't feel like the familiar house where we celebrated my birthdays and Christmases, and where I ate dinner almost every night. Mom and Dad told me to behave and not cause trouble for Mama Silvia. "We'll see you soon. Remember that we love you very much," Mom said, kissing my cheek. "Please take good care of her, Mama," my mom told my grandmother. Her eyes were full of tears.

"What other choice do I have?" Mama Silvia said.

My dad thanked my grandmother for taking me in and then put his arm around my mom as they walked out.

I wanted to run after them. I wanted to tell them not to leave me. But I couldn't move. I knew that no matter what I said or did, they were going back to America and my sisters were going to stay in their new schools. With the baby on the way, my parents didn't feel like mine anymore. I saw Dad squeeze my mom's arm as they walked down the few steps that led to the street from my grandmother's house. They didn't look back.

LA ESCOLTA

WHEN I WAS NINE, MY little brother was born on Christmas Day in San Antonio, Texas. I had been moping around because my parents didn't make it to Taxco for the holidays, and now I had received the worst news.

When my dad called to tell us, I could feel his happiness through the phone. It couldn't be contained, not even by the US-Mexico border. He sounded like he had just received the best Christmas present in the whole world.

Not only had I been kicked off the donkey, but it happened in grand fashion. The new baby was a boy *and* he was born on Christmas Day. In America. He was named after my dad, Julio, and my maternal grandfather, Miguel. He was blessed, and there was no denying it.

I didn't see my parents for months, and it seemed like no matter what I accomplished, their new miracle baby was the only thing they cared about. So, as I started fifth grade, my attitude about school completely changed. I no longer cared to be the smartest girl in class in order to impress my parents. I heard Mama Silvia on the phone with my mother one night. "Julissa is not acting like herself. She needs you, Luisa."

I got my third report card of the year in the spring, with failing grades in math and science. I loved math, and I was embarrassed that I had failed my favorite subject.

"Julissa, we'll need your grandma to sign this and come see me this week," the teacher said when she handed me the report card.

"Okay, *maestra*," I said, stuffing the piece of paper into my newest Cinderella backpack from America. I was so nervous to show my report card to Mama Silvia, and even more worried about how disappointed my parents would be. My mom had told me many times, "Learning is the most important thing you can do. My job is to work, your job is to do well in school."

That night, my grandmother and I were watching our *novelas* in her living room when I said, "Mama Silvia, I have to show you something. Please don't be mad at me."

"Ay, *mija*, you poor thing," my grandma said when I showed her my report card. She pulled me toward her and gave me a big, long hug.

When I gave my mom the news the next night, she wasn't mad at me either. She offered me a deal.

"If you make *La Escolta*, I won't miss it for the world. I will be there, I promise."

In Mexico, one of the biggest academic honors you can receive is to be part of *La Escolta*. The students march around the school while the national anthem plays, and the student with the highest GPA and best conduct gets to hold the flag.

I hadn't seen my mom in months at that point. It was all I wanted. So I took the deal. I wasn't too worried about making good grades; I knew that if I studied hard enough, I could have the highest GPA in my class. But good grades alone weren't enough. I also had to have good conduct—the one thing that repeatedly kept me out of *La Escolta*. I liked to ask my teachers questions that they found annoying, and sometimes disrespectful.

I kept my mouth closed, didn't ask any questions, and studied really hard. A girl named Evelyn beat me by one point in good conduct, so she held the flag, but I still made *La Escolta* the next grading period. The day I found out I would be marching around the school, I ran to Metales Aviles to give Mama Silvia the good news. Metales Aviles was our family business, and Mama Silvia worked there every day, even on Sundays. My mom and dad had helped build Los Metales Aviles when my grandfather was still alive. My uncles Alex and Mike were too young at the time. But once my uncles were older, they took over and my parents began building their own business.

I could tell my grandmother was really proud and happy. The truth was, I was also really happy. I loved the feeling of accomplishing a goal. In fact, over the past few months my grandma had taught me how to make my bed, how to cook eggs, and how to make a ponytail out of my thick hair. I had to endure new hurtful chants at school because it took me a few weeks to learn how to properly brush my hair. The girls at school began calling me "*la greñuda*," the girl with the messy hair. But I was so glad she was teaching me how to take care of myself.

I spoke to my mom on the phone that night.

"Mami, Mami! I made it. I made *La Escolta*," I said with happy tears. It was then that I realized I liked making good grades, not just for my parents, but also for me.

"That's so wonderful, *mija*!"

The next couple of weeks passed in a flurry of excitement. I was at Mama Silvia's house, finishing my homework and waiting for my mom to come through the door any minute. And then the phone rang.

"*Mija*, I am at the airport in Chicago, but my flight was canceled due to a snowstorm." Her voice cracked.

I had never seen snow, and it was hard to imagine any type of bad weather, because the blue sky in Taxco didn't have a single cloud.

"You can't do this to me. You promised, Mama." I couldn't believe she didn't keep her promise.

Mama Silvia came to the living room and asked what was happening.

"She isn't going to make it," I said, handing her the phone.

"Luisa, this is not right. You can't do this to her," my grandma scolded my mom.

When my grandma got off the phone with my mom, she said, "Don't worry, I'll be there tomorrow."

Why didn't my mom fly down sooner? I wondered. I was old enough to recognize that my mother was often late, messy, and disorganized. *Was she late to the airport? Is that why she missed her flight? Or was it baby Julio who was slowing her down?*

I stayed up all night, fantasizing about my mother miraculously making it to Taxco in time. The next morning, Mama Silvia blow-dried her white hair and wore her best dress. She was shaped like a pear, and none of the dresses at the stores fit her, so hers were all custom made. She wore them daily with a different color checkered apron, even if she wasn't in the kitchen cooking. She only took off the apron to go to church or if I was marching in *La Escolta*.

Mama Silvia walked with me to school and watched me march in *La Escolta*.

I marched on the wrong foot the entire time. I kept looking to the school's doorway, waiting for my mom to make a dramatic entrance, but she never did. The applause, the national anthem, and the parade meant nothing without my mom there.

I could never be what a baby boy was in my parents' eyes, but after years of lessons, I could paint, play the piano, and even make *La Escolta*. I was determined to have the best painting at the art show, the best piano performance at the recital, the most karate trophies. I wanted them to say to the other parents, "That's our daughter." I wanted them to be proud of me.

A few days later, I came home to my grandma's house after school and my mom was sitting in the living room, crying. "There was a terrible storm in Chicago, and I begged the flight attendant to let me fly anywhere. Eventually I made it to Houston and took the first flight out to Mexico City," she explained. My mom had really tried to make it. She only stayed two days and then had to return to San Antonio.

Before she left I asked her, "Mami, when is the house going to be done? When are you coming home for good?"

She sighed and said, "*Mija*, I don't know."

It was the most honest answer she had ever given me.

BACK TO AMERICA

ONE DAY TOWARD THE END of fifth grade, as I was putting my clean clothes in the drawers of my room, I found a magazine for adults. My room had been my uncle's before I moved in with Mama Silvia, and since I kept most of my belongings at our apartment on La Calle Nueva, I hadn't used the drawers much before. But for the past couple of weeks, Aris and Nay had stayed in Cuernavaca to study for their final exams, so I had brought extra clothes to Mama Silvia's house. When I found the magazine, I decided to give it to Enrique, a boy in my art class who I had a crush on even though he was a teenager and I was only ten. He had light-colored skin, like my mom's, and hazel eyes. I wrapped the magazine in a newspaper and hid it in my backpack. I was so excited that he would think I was cool.

Enrique had been really nice to me since I joined the art school a few years back, helping me carry heavy equipment when we worked with ceramics, and often complimenting my artwork. I had resolved to stop being sad that my parents were always away and instead focus on making new friends.

That day Enrique was sitting across from me in art class. We were working with oil on canvas; I was painting a vase with flowers. I waited until the teacher wasn't looking, and then ran around the table and whispered that I had something to give him after class.

In my excitement, I knocked over my own painting, which was still wet, and it was pretty much ruined when it hit the floor, but I didn't care. Enrique would think I was supercool. I was sure of it.

When class was over, I went up to him and said, "Wait right here. I'm going to get something for you."

I made my way to my backpack and took out my gift. I ran back to where he was standing and handed him the bundle of newspaper.

"What is this?" he asked.

"Just take a look," I said, smiling from ear to ear. He looked at the magazine, and his eyes widened in disbelief.

"Maestra Estela!" he yelled, and ran all the way down the hall to the teacher's office. I didn't understand what was happening. A couple of minutes later, Maestra Estela called me into her office, and I passed Enrique as I walked in. He looked shaken, and his eyes were watery.

"Where did you get this?" Maestra Estela asked me. It hadn't occurred to me that I might be in trouble for giving this gift to Enrique. I didn't want to get my uncle into trouble since I'd found it in his old room, so I refused to answer.

"I don't know," I kept repeating.

"I am calling your grandmother," she said. "You can go home now."

I didn't want to go to Mama Silvia's house. I wasn't sure why I was in trouble, but I knew I had done something very bad. It hadn't occurred to me that the magazine I gave to Enrique was an inappropriate gift.

Mama Silvia was sitting at the dining room table when I walked in the front door. She said, "I already called your mother. She is on her way back to Taxco.

Your sisters will be here tomorrow. Everyone needs to be home with you right now."

She had a rosary in her hand and she told me she was praying extra rosaries for me that night. Within a few days, both my parents flew back to Mexico. Everyone told me they were sorry for leaving me alone so often and blamed themselves for my bad behavior. No one ever explained to me what I had done that was so wrong.

But one day, while I lay down to take a nap in our apartment on La Calle Nueva, I overheard my mother talking with one of her close friends on the phone. "Aris and Nay are such good daughters," she said. "I don't know where we went wrong with Julissa."

I was so confused. A few days later, my parents went back to the United States, and I thought the whole ordeal was over.

When summer came, I flew to San Antonio with my sisters to visit my parents, just as I had many times before. Before the new school year started, both of my sisters flew back to Mexico, but I didn't.

I was sitting in my parents' living room playing with baby Julio. He had grown a lot in the past few months, since the first time I met him, when he couldn't even sit up. He was playing with a toy fire truck, and I was pushing it around him when my dad said, "*Mija*, come over here. Your mom and I want to talk to you."

It turned out that ever since I had given that magazine to Enrique, my parents had been making plans to have me live with them in the United States. They were so worried I might go down the wrong path.

"You are not flying back to Mexico. You are staying with us."

PART
2

SWEET HOME TEXAS

IN A WHIPLASH, MY ENTIRE life changed. I had wished for so long to be a family, but this was not how I had dreamt it. I had a home in a new country, but without Mama Silvia, Nay, or Aris. Everything happened so fast that I didn't even get a chance to say good-bye to anyone in Taxco.

A couple of days after my parents told me America was my new home, my mom flew off to a trade show. Dad, Julio, and I drove Mom and Sam to the airport. I had met Sam the first time I visited the United States. He was traveling with my mom to help her work at the trade show. My dad stayed behind to take care of Julio and me.

"I'll be back on Wednesday. Take care of Julio while I am gone," Mom said above the intercom noise announcing departure gates.

She leaned down and gave me a kiss, and then kissed Julio's chubby cheeks while he sat in his stroller. Julio, who was eighteen months old, started crying when he saw Mom walk away toward the gate.

"It's okay, Julio, don't cry," I said, picking him up from his stroller.

Nay had been the one to comfort me when Mom left for the *ferias*, and now it was my turn to comfort my baby brother.

Mom looked back before boarding the plane and blew us a kiss.

☆

A couple of weeks later, we were sitting at the dining room table having breakfast when my mom said, "We found a great Catholic school for you to attend when the new school year starts."

"Is it a bilingual school?" I asked.

"I don't know. We are going to visit the school, and we'll ask then," she said.

My parents didn't speak English fluently. They had learned how to speak to their customers about sterling silver, and Sam often served as their translator at the trade shows. But it didn't stop my mom from asking dozens of questions the day we went to Sacred Heart so I could be enrolled in their sixth-grade class.

The Catholic school was much bigger than my school had been in Mexico. We walked into the admissions office and my mom said, "We take daughter to school." My dad mostly kept quiet around anyone he didn't know, even if they spoke Spanish. When the receptionist couldn't understand my mom, she unabashedly started using her hands, pointing at me and saying, "She go to school here."

While my mom filled out the paperwork, she looked nervously at my dad.

"It's asking for a social security number," she said to him.

My dad said it shouldn't matter that I didn't have a social security number since this wasn't a public school.

My parents had brought me to America on a tourist visa instead of a student visa. Enrolling me in school was a violation of that permit, even if I was going to a private school. If immigration somehow found out I was using a tourist visa, I could have been sent back to Mexico and separated from my parents.

The principal must have known I was on a tourist visa, since a copy of my passport was made, but she agreed that since this was a private school, they could enroll me without a social security number.

Sacred Heart didn't offer ESL (English as a second language) courses. Even if they did, my mom would have never enrolled me in such classes. There was—and still is—a feeling of shame that if you didn't speak English, it meant you weren't smart. This is not true, of course, but appearances are everything in America. Somehow *ESL* means "remedial" to a lot of people, when it should just mean "I speak one more language than you do." I had taken some English lessons in Mexico, but they taught me very little. I could sing one song in English. That was it.

"I don't speak English. How can I go to school here? I won't be able to make any friends," I protested.

"It's what's best for you, Julissa," Mom said. "You'll learn English soon enough. It's a great school, and you will get the best education."

Before moving to San Antonio, I imagined that

classrooms in America were filled with only rich, beautiful white kids like I'd seen on TV. But that wasn't my experience. On the first day of school I got dressed in my uniform: a maroon skirt, white blouse, and maroon necktie. Both Mom and Dad drove me to school, but only my mom took me to the front office. A teacher named Ms. Garcia was waiting for me.

"*Hola, Julissa, que gusto conocerte,*" she said.

I was so relieved that my teacher spoke Spanish and that she was glad to meet me.

"Come, I'll take you to the classroom," she said.

"I'll be back to pick you up this afternoon," Mom said.

I walked nervously behind Ms. Garcia. Once we arrived at the classroom, she showed me to my desk. I sat quietly and observed as a few brown kids with black hair, who looked liked me, also walked into the classroom. There were a couple of Black kids and Asian kids too. Once the bell rang, all the kids stood up to recite the morning prayer and the Pledge of Allegiance. I didn't know what my classmates were saying, but I put my right hand over my heart and faced the US flag like I was one of them.

After everyone was seated, Ms. Garcia made an announcement. I couldn't understand anything she was saying, but I heard my name and the words *Mexico* and *Spanish* in the announcement. I imagined she was telling my classmates that my name was Julissa, I came from Mexico, and I spoke only Spanish. After the announcement, Ms. Garcia called a girl named Brittany to the front of the classroom. After speaking with Brittany, Ms. Garcia called me to her desk.

"This is Brittany. She is going to be your buddy," she said.

I was confused. There were lots of other kids in my classroom who I thought spoke Spanish since they looked like me. Why was my buddy a girl who probably didn't speak Spanish?

"*Hola, soy Brittany. Bienvenida*," the girl said, welcoming me.

My eyes grew big in surprise. Ms. Garcia noticed and said, "Brittany is the only person in our classroom who speaks Spanish."

"Hi," I said, embarrassed.

I had assumed she didn't speak Spanish because she was blond and had green eyes. Later, when people made assumptions about me because I have brown skin and black hair, I'd try to be forgiving, reminding myself that I had made that mistake once too.

Brittany was the most popular girl in our classroom. During lunch I sat at a table with Brittany and her friends, but I couldn't join in the conversation. I laughed when the other girls laughed, but I had no idea what was so funny. After we finished lunch, Brittany asked if it was okay if she left with her friends. I said, "*¡Claro!*" Of course she could go with her friends; she wasn't my baby-sitter, after all.

It was then, when I was sitting alone at a picnic table by the playground, that a Latina girl with curly hair and braces came up to me. "I am Tiffani," she pointed to herself.

"*Yo estoy* in your class," she said. She was also new to the school. Tiffani and I spent the rest of recess trying to understand each other, and laughing at our funny-sounding Spanglish. I found a new buddy. Tiffani may not have spoken Spanish, and I didn't speak English, but we understood each other. She became my first real friend.

I waited after school as cars pulled up to pick up my

classmates. I was nervous that my parents might be late, but after a few minutes I saw their black SUV pull up. My dad was driving, my mom was in the passenger seat, and Julio was in his car seat in the back. My entire family was picking me up!

"How was school?" Mom asked.

"It was okay. I made a friend, but I didn't understand a single word anyone said."

"It's okay, *mija*. You'll learn English fast. You are very smart," my dad added. My parents hired Ms. Garcia to tutor me every day after class and on weekends, so I could start learning English as soon as possible. In their eyes this wasn't about fitting in; it was a matter of survival. But, other than the language barrier, for the most part, I felt like I could be happy living in America.

DIFFERENT

I HAD NEVER FELT SO dumb in my life. Even when I had failing grades in Mexico, I knew it was because I wasn't trying. In my new school, I worked very hard to learn English and keep up with the material.

"I failed a test where I could look at the book for answers. Mom is going to be mad," I said to my dad one day, feeling defeated.

"She knows you are doing your best. Keep working hard and you will do better," my dad said.

Mom was only home Tuesdays through Thursdays most weeks; the rest of the time she was traveling to cities across the United States for trade shows so she could pay for my tuition, our bills, and my sisters' education back in Mexico. Aris had two years left to get her degree, and then Nay would start college. I wished it was my dad who traveled instead, but my mom was a much better salesperson.

My bad grades weren't my only problem at school. One day, I was sitting with Brittany and her friends when I took out the lunch that my dad had packed for me: two hard-boiled eggs and cucumber salad. He thought a school lunch of corn dogs or pizza was garbage and bad for my health. One of the girls said something about eggs being stinky, from what I could understand. All the girls laughed and waved their hands in front of their faces to make the smell go away. As usual, I laughed, except this time, I was laughing at myself.

"You know they were laughing at you, right?" Tiffani said at recess.

"No way! I don't believe you. You weren't even sitting with us," I told Tiffani.

Tiffani wasn't invited to sit at Brittany's table. She sat at a table a couple of rows behind us, and I thought she was jealous because I sat with the popular girls and she didn't. But as my vocabulary grew, I began to understand what the girls said during lunch, and soon realized Tiffani had been telling the truth.

"Look at her with her Pocahontas hair. Her food smells terrible. I don't know why she sits here," a girl named Melissa said.

"My hair is pretty," I responded to Melissa.

Her eyes grew big in disbelief.

"I understand everything you say," I added, and got up from the table.

I quickly walked to the girls' bathroom down the hall. Once I was safely inside the bathroom stall, I let out the tears I'd been holding back.

"I am sorry I didn't believe you," I said to Tiffani, who had followed me to the bathroom when she had seen I was upset.

"It's okay. We can sit together now," she said.

She didn't mind my stinky eggs and cucumber salad. And when she laughed at something, she explained it to me so I could understand why it was funny. I was happy to have a best friend in Tiffani, but I missed Nay terribly. She had always stood up for me, but now I had to stand up for myself. I was happy to finally live with my parents, but in many ways, my daily life had been better in Mexico. At least in Taxco, I spoke the same language as everyone else. I was one of the smart girls in class. And even if it got me in trouble, I always felt comfortable saying what was on my mind.

In America, I struggled to form even one complete sentence. Although the kids at school made fun of me for being different, I didn't let their ridicule shut me down. I continued to raise my hand in class. I learned how to be strong from my mom. She was never embarrassed when she spoke English, and if people didn't understand her, she would try again and again until they did.

☆

I was so happy when Clara joined our class a few months into the school year. She was from Spain, and had just moved to Texas. Even though she spoke English fluently, she also spoke Spanish. Tiffani and I immediately introduced ourselves, and volunteered to show her around the school. I hoped that my number of friends would grow from one to two.

My parents normally didn't let me spend time at other kids' houses. But since Clara's parents spoke Spanish, they convinced my mom to let me visit their home. My dad drove me to Clara's house one Saturday. She lived in a gated community with houses that were much bigger than the houses where the really rich girls in Taxco lived.

"Wow, you didn't tell me your friend was rich," my dad said as we drove past mansion after mansion.

"I didn't know either," I said.

The entrance to her home was beautiful. A staircase led to the second floor and a huge chandelier hung from the tall ceiling. Clara spent most of the day showing me her many toys and her closet full of pretty clothes, and telling me about all the places she visited around the world.

Before my dad picked me up, she said, "Why are you friends with Tiffani? She is so loud."

"She's my best friend. I like that she is loud."

I admired Tiffani for not caring what the girls said about her at school. She never tried to fit in. If someone didn't like her, she thought it was their problem, not hers.

"You should come sit with Brittany and me at lunch on Monday," Clara said.

I had sat with the popular girls before, and I didn't like it.

"It's okay. I am going to sit with Tiffani," I responded.

Clara and I only had the Spanish language in

common. Soon, she joined in with the same group of girls who made fun of me. As our sixth-grade year came to a close, Clara had a going-away party at her parents' mansion. Her dad had been transferred again to a different country, and she would not be coming back the next school year. The house was decorated like something out of a fairy tale. She changed into three different beautiful outfits and made grand entrances in each of them during the party. Everyone had such fun.

I didn't witness any of this with my own eyes, though. I heard about it all from the other students. Tiffani and I were the only two girls in the entire class who weren't invited. I tried not to let it bother me, thinking one day I would have a *quinceañera*, and I would be the one in a beautiful dress.

When the last day of school finally came, I was glad the year was over.

A DARKER SIDE

THE SUMMER AFTER SIXTH GRADE, my parents enrolled me in intensive English classes, stretching their budget and working extra trade shows so they could afford to send me. So off I went from 9:00 AM to 3:00 PM every day, all summer long—not with students my age, but with adults. There were eight levels in the English program, and thanks to all the tutoring I'd had during sixth grade, I tested into level five. I was glad I tested so high, because I didn't want my parents to spend more money than necessary.

I noticed my dad's shoes had a small hole in them when

he picked me up from my English classes. "Dad, you need new shoes," I said. I hated seeing my parents struggle.

"They are fine, *mija*. This way my feet get some air," he said, laughing.

Seeing my parents stressed over money made me feel guilty about all the trouble I caused back in Taxco. I couldn't help but feel that my presence only made things more difficult for them. With me around, my dad couldn't travel with my mom, and they couldn't work two different trade shows at the same time like they did before. Julio used to travel with my parents like I did when I went to the *ferias* with them as a little girl. Having a nanny stay with us wasn't an option since they were so much more expensive to have than in Mexico.

Maybe it was also my fault that they fought almost every night. I hadn't said anything to my parents, but I could hear their arguments through my bedroom door.

"We don't have money for that!" my dad would shout.

"I am not taking the girls out of their schools. We will just have to work harder," my mom responded.

I could hear their voices getting louder and louder through my bedroom door. Sometimes, I could hear things being thrown. But I stayed in my bed, pretending that I had a perfect, happy family. I had wished for so long to live with my parents that I didn't want to complain about anything.

When my parents visited me in Taxco, my dad was always the fun parent. He taught me how to ride a bike, took me to soccer games, showed me the proper way to eat tacos al pastor, and always made me laugh. I don't remember the first time he hit me, but I do remember the first really bad beating. My mom was away at a trade show, so I had to help my dad with Julio. I was in the kitchen trying to open up a can of liquid baby formula for his bottle. The can slipped from my hand, and the formula spilled everywhere, splashing on the floor and cabinets.

When dad walked into the kitchen, he saw the mess and started yelling. He grabbed a wooden spoon that was near the stove and began hitting me with it.

"Do you know how much that baby formula costs?" my dad screamed.

Julio cried hysterically when he saw me cry and wince from the pain. I told my dad I was sorry, but it didn't help.

"Please stop! Please stop," I kept crying as I put my hands up to cover my face. But he didn't stop until the spoon broke.

He grabbed another can from the pantry and finished making Julio a bottle. He picked up my baby brother and tenderly fed him the bottle. I stayed frozen in the kitchen. I didn't know what to do.

"I am so sorry, *mija*. I don't know what came over me," he said after he put Julio to sleep.

"It's okay, Dad. It's okay."

I knew my parents were under a lot of stress, and I tried to understand. My dad had a hard life growing up, so I convinced myself that it wasn't his fault he had lost his temper.

When I first moved in with my parents, I noticed that my dad would drink a beer or two every night. As the school year went on, those two beers turned into six beers, and then more than that. He never drank during the day. He never picked me up from school after drinking. But every night, he got drunk. And the more he drank, the more he yelled, and the more he hit.

When Mom came home, she saw a bruise the wooden spoon had left on my arm.

"What happened to you?" she asked.

I told her what had happened, and she stormed into her room and screamed at my dad.

"Don't you ever hit her again!" she yelled.

That night they fought again about money, about his drinking, about him hitting me, about him being tired of being home alone with two kids instead of working at the trade shows.

Dad would always apologize after hitting me. He would tell me he was sorry and that he'd never do it again, and I knew he *wanted* to never hit me again. But he did. My mom would yell at him, and they would argue. I tried to do everything perfectly, so I wouldn't upset him. But no matter what I did, it would happen all over again.

One morning after my mom had left for another trade show, I made eggs for breakfast and burned them. The smoke filled the kitchen and made it look like a foggy day.

My dad walked into the kitchen and told me to eat them.

"But they're burned!" I cried.

"Then you should have been paying more attention!"

he yelled, forcing me to swallow the charred, blackened, disgusting mess I'd made.

Afterward he apologized again, but I was becoming more scared of him with each passing day.

That same weekend I tried making eggs again. I wanted to show my dad that I was capable of cooking. I was a nervous wreck, and accidentally threw the eggs into the pan so hard that the oil splashed on my forearm. Bubbles formed on my skin.

I hid the burn by wearing a long-sleeved shirt so my dad wouldn't see it.

Later that day, Julio and I were playing outside at the apartment complex while my dad was grilling dinner. It was one of those hot Texas summer days.

"Why are you wearing that shirt? Aren't you hot?" my dad asked me.

"No, no, no. I'm okay," I said.

Then he touched my arm, and saw me wince.

"What's the matter?" he asked, and I showed him.

"Oh my God. Why didn't you tell me?" he said, concerned.

I started crying, "I thought you'd be mad at me."

"I'm so sorry," he said. "Of course I'm not mad."

He cleaned my arm, put Neosporin on the burn, and took care of my wound. He was really loving and understanding about it. When I got up to wash the dishes after our barbecue, he told me to stay put. "I'll take care of the dishes tonight."

FITTING IN AND
STANDING OUT

I HAD BEEN LIVING IN San Antonio for over a year, and during that time I rarely talked to my sisters. Phone calls to Mexico were expensive. Whenever my parents made calls to Taxco, they did so to speak to Mama Silvia about money for my sisters. I felt the distance between my family in Mexico and my life in America getting bigger with each passing day.

I often had very vivid dreams about Mama Silvia's

green parrot, my *quinceañera*, and Aris and Nay, or about running around the streets of Taxco with my cousins. I would dream about all the things I had left behind in Taxco. One weekend in the seventh grade, I had a dream where I was in our apartment on La Calle Nueva. Cande, my beloved nanny, was there. When she walked into the kitchen I said, "Hi, Cande. It's so good to see you," and I ran to hug her.

She responded, "I've missed you so much."

I woke up and realized I had dreamt in English. I was excited and scared.

What if I forget how to speak Spanish?

I didn't want to let go of my Mexican roots while living my American life. The rest of the weekend I jammed to Juan Gabriel and José Alfredo Jiménez, two of the most influential musicians in Mexican history. Instead of watching American television shows, I spent the weekend watching Univision and Telemundo, two Spanish-speaking channels. Dad asked if I wanted to go to McDonald's for lunch and I said, "No, I want Mexican food."

He smiled and said, "Let's go to Rosario's."

My mom was away at another trade show. My dad ordered a burrito and I ordered chicken tacos.

When the tacos came to the table, I said, "What is this? This isn't Mexican food."

They were hard-shell tacos with yellow cheese on top of the chicken. I was expecting soft corn tortillas, onions, and cilantro.

"This is Tex-Mex food," my dad said. "Try it, you'll like it."

I took a bite and sure enough, the tacos were delicious. It was Mexican food with an American twist, and I was okay with that. Maybe it was fine that I spoke English in my dreams, because I still spoke Spanish every day with my mom and dad.

I had been so worried that I was becoming too American because I had one dream in English, but I soon found out that to some people, speaking English was not enough to belong.

On Monday morning, my teacher announced the names of the students who would be placed in the honors math class for seventh grade, and I was so happy to hear my name. Throughout sixth grade, math was the only class where I didn't feel stupid. Two plus two is four in any language. Most of the topics I was learning, I'd already come across in fourth grade in Mexico.

Justin was not in the honors class. He was a white kid with freckles who rarely even looked my way. I had exchanged a few words with him once, when we were on the same dodgeball team in gym class.

"Why is *she* in the honors class?" he said. Then he said slowly, "She's *a Mex-i-can*. She doesn't even speak English!"

The whole class laughed.

"Justin!" The teacher called out.

"I speak English. I am also better at math than you are."

My classmates responded with an "Ooohhh!"

"That's enough!" the teacher said, and called us both to her desk.

"Justin, apologize to Julissa."

"Why? It's true; she is a Mexican," he said.

My face was hot with anger.

"I am Mexican, and I am good at math. Not like you, dummy!" I yelled.

"Julissa, stop it! No name calling!"

We were both in trouble. I thought I was defending myself, but calling Justin a dummy was apparently just as offensive as him saying I couldn't do math because I was Mexican.

When my dad picked me up from school, I let out all the tears I had been holding in the whole day. "I want to go back to Mexico where I can be Mexican with everyone else," I said.

"What happened, *mija*?" he asked.

I told him about Justin's hurtful words and getting in trouble for calling him a dummy.

"I am glad you stood up for yourself. Don't pay attention to what he said," my dad said. "It will be all right."

But once my eyes were opened to the racism around me, I could never close them again. I had dismissed Melissa's bullying about my stinky eggs and long "Pocahontas" hair as just comments from a mean girl. But did I not fit in because I was a Mexican? Was *that* the reason I had such a hard time making friends?

My parents never really spoke to me about race or racism. I don't know if they ever experienced it, if they were unaware of it, or if they thought it no longer happened in America. When I told my mom about Justin's comments, she dismissed it as a comment from a mean boy.

As the weeks passed in seventh grade, I learned about the history of racism in America and the civil rights movement in class, and it made a deep emotional impression on me. But my schoolbooks taught racism as a dynamic exclusively between white and Black people.

I'd share everything I learned with my dad on our rides home after school, and with my mom when she'd come home from her trade shows.

"I can't believe they treated Black people so badly," I told my mom one day during dinner. "I can't believe you brought me to a country that *owned* people!" I later learned that Mexico also had slaves, but *that* history had been left out of my Mexican history books.

"*Mija*, that was a long time ago," she said.

"Racism still happens, Mom. Did you forget what Justin said to me?"

"Learn what you need to learn, do well on your tests, but don't let it affect you so much."

I might not have read about Mexicans in the US history books in school, but I knew instantly that Justin saw me in the same way so many people viewed Black people in American history: as less than. I realized that being Mexican was something bad in his eyes. Everything in his voice and expression told me he saw me as an outsider. And it hurt. I wasn't like everyone else. I wasn't white. I wasn't Black. I was *a Mexican*.

CHEERS!

"I AM GOING TO TRY out for the cheerleading squad," I told Tiffani at recess toward the end of seventh grade.

I wanted to join the drama club, but the cool kids in my school didn't act in plays. They played sports. They were cheerleaders. I wanted to keep my Mexican roots, but I also craved fitting in and being accepted.

"I have been thinking of trying out too," she said.

Tiffani had taken gymnastics since she was a little girl, and she could do a lot more acrobatic moves than I could. I was excited at the possibility of both of us being cheerleaders. We practiced our routines together after school at her home. When tryouts finally came, I walked into the gym wearing my physical education uniform: maroon shorts and a white T-shirt. I didn't know that girls wore tights and leotards with ribbons in their hair for tryouts. It never occurred to me to ask Tiffani what I should wear. I felt so out of place. My classmates were on the gym floor stretching, and they all looked at me like I was from another planet. I saw Tiffani and ran to her.

"I look so stupid," I said.

"Who cares what you are wearing? What matters is how you cheer and dance. Plus, you have really good grades, and the teacher likes you," she added.

In order to make the cheerleading squad, I had to do well in the audition, but the overall score included points for good grades and excellent conduct. I thought about all the times I didn't make *La Escolta* back in Mexico because of my conduct. But in Texas, I didn't speak out of turn since I was still somewhat hesitant due to my accent. I tried to stay positive, but my face was burning with embarrassment, as the girls were pointing at me and giggling.

One by one, my classmates were called into the dance studio to try out.

When it was my turn, Mrs. Smith, the dance teacher, said, "Come on in; do the best you can."

And I did. I did the best I could. I cheered loudly and with sharp moves. I jumped as high as I could. I made up for my outfit with a bright smile.

The next day during gym class the results were posted on a sheet of paper outside Mrs. Smith's office. The names were in alphabetical order, and since my last name starts with an *A*, I immediately saw it on the list.

"I made the squad!" I said to Tiffani, who was standing next to me.

She looked at the list for a couple of minutes and said, "I didn't make it."

"How is that possible? You can do back handsprings."

"The teacher hates me, and my grades aren't so great. Oh well," Tiffani said, disappointed.

I was sad too. It didn't seem fair that I had made the squad and Tiffani had not. Mrs. Smith offered Tiffani a captain position on the pom squad instead. I was glad that Tiffani would be in the stands at the Friday-night football games cheering for the team, while I was on the field with the other cheerleaders.

Before I could officially join the team, I had to get a permission form signed by my parents. I was at home filling out the form: name, address, and phone number, all pretty standard. But then there was a field for a social security number.

"Mom, what's my social security number?"

"Why?" she asked in a serious voice.

I explained that I needed it to join the cheerleading team. Then she said that I didn't have a social security number, but that it shouldn't matter because the principal had been fine with me enrolling in school without one.

"Why can't you get me one?" I asked.

"It's not that simple. I'll talk to your teacher in the morning."

My mom also told me I shouldn't tell people that I didn't have a social security number. A visa was all that mattered. My mom spoke to the cheerleading coach, and I was allowed to join the team.

I spent the first half of the summer before eighth grade going to cheerleading practice and trying to bond with the other cheerleaders. Some of our practices were held at Melissa's house, the girl who'd made fun of my lunch in sixth grade. I spoke English fluently, but I still had a hard time with common expressions.

One afternoon, we were in her backyard practicing a cheer, and Melissa said, "Break a leg!"

I responded with "That is so mean!"

She started laughing and said, "No, dummy! It means good luck."

I never quite bonded with the other cheerleaders. At every practice, I wished Tiffani had made the squad. I hoped Nay could move to Texas to live with us, but she was starting college soon and on the rare occasions we spoke on the phone she would say, "My life is in Mexico."

I also felt guilty because the uniforms and cheerleading camp were so expensive, and no matter how hard my parents worked, they were still struggling with money.

"Mami, I can quit the team," I told her one morning after I heard my parents fight about the price of the cheerleading uniform.

"No, *mija*, you like it. It's part of being young and making friends," she said. "You'll come with me to some of the trade shows this summer, and you can help me work, okay?"

I was so happy she let me stay on the cheerleading squad. In my uniform, watching and cheering for our football team, I felt like an all-American girl. It was during those Friday nights that I fell in love with football. I loved learning about the plays, the formations, and all the details of the game. When I was on the field cheering for our team, I could forget about my dad's temper, my parents' money problems, and my accent, and just be a normal teenager.

In my uniform, on the football field, I felt like I belonged. Someone like me, with no social security number, strong cultural roots, and an accent could be both: Mexican *and* American.

ON THE ROAD WITH MOM

I SPENT THE REST OF the summer working with my mom at trade shows. Now that I spoke English I helped as her translator, and she saved money by not having Sam work at each show. The trade shows were just as I remembered. They took place at big convention centers in cities like New Orleans, Houston, and Dallas. Inside were rows and rows of vendor booths, selling everything from clothes to sunglasses to jewelry.

I loved seeing my mom walk with a confidence that I didn't see when she was home in San Antonio. She was very outgoing, full of energy, and happy. And she never, ever gave up.

At the end of one trade show that summer, we were packing the boxes and suitcases of jewelry into a van. There were still many boxes left that wouldn't fit.

"There's no more room," I complained.

"There is always a solution to everything," she said.

She took the boxes and suitcases out of the van and started over again, arranging them in different ways. I stood next to the van, exhausted from the weekend, but my mom got every single box to fit. And that was how she approached everything. Over and over again I watched my mom persevere and figure things out when others would have quit.

My mom was charming. Whether she needed to get to the front of a long line because we were in a hurry or wanted a discount on a purchase she was making, she was able to talk her way into or out of things. Sometimes her boldness would embarrass me. I wished that when somebody said no, she would just say, "Okay," and move on. But most of the time when we heard no, I shook my head and instantly thought, *Here we go. . . .*

Traveling with her was the only time I really got to see her, so I didn't want to complain too much. But I asked her, "Mom, why doesn't Dad come to the trade shows, and you stay home with Julio and me?"

"I like coming to the trade shows. I am good at selling. You know your dad isn't very good with people."

She was a much better salesperson because she had an outgoing personality. It made sense. That night when we got back to the hotel, I just wanted to go to sleep. I didn't want to brush my teeth or wash my face. It had been a long day of work. My mom, on the other hand, took some cream and put it on her face, then wiped it off. Then she washed her face with facial soap, and put on another cream. She said the worst insult you can make to yourself is to go to sleep with a dirty face. I got up from bed and washed my face too.

I have always considered my mom stunningly beautiful, and I wanted to look like her. When I was little, I used to admire the way Aris put her makeup on, and now I had my mom to look up to. So I paid attention to the way she took care of herself. The next day at the show, my mom asked, "*Mija*, can we pierce your ears?"

I didn't want to pierce my ears because I thought it would hurt. I had gotten my ears pierced as a baby, but my ears got infected and the holes closed.

My mom said, "A girl without earrings is like a night without stars."

I let her pierce my ears that morning. To this day, if I ever forget to wear earrings, I feel like a night without stars. I started imitating my mom during the trade shows. A woman was trying on some earrings and she didn't seem sure she was going to buy them. I looked at her and said, "A girl without earrings is like a night without stars, and those are beautiful stars on you."

"Awww," she said.

She bought five pairs of earrings.

Mom looked at me and smiled.

I loved spending time with my mom at the trade shows. If my life could have been all about going to school, traveling with my mom, and buying and selling silver, I think living in America would have been a lot easier. Life at home with my dad was still so confusing.

Dad and Mom (second and third from the left)
surrounded by family on their Catholic wedding day

Cutting my cake during my
presentacion de los tres años

Me during picture day
in kindergarten

At age four with my mom and
cousin Jessi (left)

At age four posing for the camera before my ballet recital

At age seven with my mom, my dad, Nay (back row, middle), a cousins during a school festival

Me, Mami, Nay, and Aris (left to right) during
a birthday party at Mama Silvia's house

At Six Flags during
my first visit to the
United States

La Escolta in fifth grade

Me in sixth grade in my basketball uniform with Julio (left) and my new neighbors

Dad and me at
the apartment in
San Antonio, Texas

The Theodore Roosevelt High School Patriots
dance team when I was in eleventh grade

The cheerleading squad in eighth grade

Me in eleventh grade during homecoming
with a fellow dance team member

High school graduation with Julio, Aris, Mom (holding my nephew Victor), and Tio Mike (left to right)

Working the funnel cake stand with Mom and Aris

THE MORE THINGS
CHANGE, THE MORE THEY
STAY THE SAME

I REALLY MISSED MY MOM when she was away. Especially the first time I got my period. Dad picked me up from school, and on the ride home he noticed I was more quiet than usual and asked, "What's wrong?" I was too embarrassed to tell my dad about it. But by the time we got home, I could barely make it up the carpeted flight of stairs that led to our apartment.

"What's wrong, *mija*?" my dad asked again, worried.

Julio was about three years old, but even as a toddler he could tell something was wrong.

"*Sana, sana, colita de rana*," Julio said when he saw me hunched over, sitting on the stairs.

I laughed at hearing him sing a lullaby parents use to soothe their kids.

"Dad, I have to tell you something."

My dad's eyes got really big.

"Tell me," he said with a serious look.

"I got my period," I said, covering my face with my hands.

"Oh! Let's take you to the store to buy what you need."

He helped me up the stairs and poured me a glass of water. He handed me an Advil and told me to lie down for a bit. When we got to the grocery store, I said, "Dad, I don't want to go inside to buy them. I wish Mom was here."

"It's a normal thing. Don't be embarrassed," he said, while he got Julio out of his car seat.

"Please, Dad, please don't make me go," I said, with my seat belt still on.

He went into the store without me and came back with a bag full of a dozen different types of sanitary napkins.

From that moment on, my dad would buy them for me every month, while I avoided facing the store clerk.

That night when Mom called us, I told her how Dad had taken care of me. He was the one who took me to school and woke up at five in the morning so I could get to cheerleading practice. He picked me up every day. He showed me how to cook and drive.

Right after my thirteenth birthday, my dad started giving me driving lessons. My cousins in Mexico had all learned how to drive when they turned fourteen. My dad didn't want me to drive in the street, but he was excited to teach me. So we started doing laps around our apartment complex.

I would sit in the driver's seat, put my seat belt on, check the mirrors before backing out of the parking spot, and listen attentively to each word my dad said.

"Never, ever, ever use your left foot, because you can get confused on what pedal to use," he would tell me. "And keep both hands on the wheel."

He was very patient when he was teaching me things, and I loved that he wanted me to know everything a father would teach a son, just like when I was a little girl.

He said if I was going to drive I needed to learn how

to fix a flat tire, how to change the oil, and what questions to ask a mechanic.

I wished he could have been like that always. He was such a wonderful dad, most of the time. He was always there to solve any problem. He told us jokes and did goofy dances just to make us laugh.

He was really fun—until he wasn't.

I wrote in my journal, *My dad hits me every day. I feel like I'm walking on eggshells, not knowing what's going to set him off.*

Every time my dad hit me, I would run to my mom or tell her over the phone when she called. My parents would get in big arguments about it. "Stop hitting her," my mom would order him, and my dad would answer in a shamed voice, "Yeah, I know." But nothing changed.

Sam lived in the same apartment complex as we did, and when my dad hit me, I would run to his apartment and tell him about it.

"I'll talk to your mom. Your dad shouldn't treat you this way," he would say. Sam became like an uncle to me.

Despite my mom's ability to fix any situation, she never could get Dad to stop hitting me. Instead, she would come home from every trip with a big smile on her face and an armful of presents for Julio and me. I know she felt she was living up to her responsibility as a parent by providing food and shelter. She thought she was going above and beyond by buying us nice things. I know she believed in her heart that she was doing her best by working so hard to provide us with the opportunity to have a better future. But she never understood it wasn't her presents that I wanted. I only *needed* her.

FRIDAY NIGHT LIGHTS

"THAT SKIRT IS TOO SHORT," Dad said when he saw me dressed in my cheerleading uniform for the first time. "I am not taking you to school wearing that."

One benefit of being a cheerleader was that on Fridays we could wear our cheerleading uniforms the entire day.

"Mom!" I screamed.

"Julio, it's a cheerleading outfit, not a nun's uniform," my mom said to my dad.

My parents fought about it, but in the end my dad agreed to let me wear the uniform to school. My mom was leaving that afternoon for another trade show, so she'd miss my first game, but she promised to come to some games during the football season to see me cheer.

The plan was for me to go to Tiffani's house after school, and my dad would pick me up after the game. I was surprised to see my dad pull up at the pickup line after school.

"Dad, did you forget? I am going to Tiffani's house, and her parents are bringing us to the game."

"Get in the car," he said.

I looked at Tiffani and shrugged my shoulders, not knowing what was going on.

"I'll see you at the game," I said to Tiffani.

When we got home, my dad said I wouldn't be going to the game wearing such a short skirt that sat right above my knees. I hoped he would change his mind before it was time for the game. But he didn't. I had been looking forward to our first football game of the season the whole summer.

"I hate you!" I yelled at him after dinner when he still refused to take me to the game.

On Monday morning, I was dreading going to school and having to explain to Mrs. Smith why I wasn't at the game.

"My dad was sick, and he couldn't drive me," I said to her during the morning practice.

"I'll need to talk to your parents. Next time you can call one of your teammates and ask for a ride."

When my mom got back from the trade show, she went to my school and spoke to Mrs. Smith. I soon found out that if my dad was in any kind of bad mood, he would refuse to take me to the football games, leaving my mom to make excuses to my coach, begging her to let me stay on the team.

My mom started lying to my dad instead by saying I was going to the trade shows with her. I couldn't miss too much school, so on those occasions I would spend a few days at Tiffani's house. I would pack a bag with normal clothes, and in the middle of the suitcase pack my school uniform and my cheerleading uniform. My mom would drive me to Tiffani's house and then take off to her next trade show.

On the day of homecoming, I couldn't risk missing the game. So my mom told my dad I would be working at a trade show.

"She is missing too much school, Luisa."

"She is keeping up with her homework. She'll be fine,"

my mom responded as she finished packing the silver jewelry.

This was the fourth trade show I "worked" with my mom during the fall.

"What's really going on here? Sam is going to the show with you, so why does she need to go too?" Dad asked.

I was sitting in the living room playing with my brother, Julio, and I exchanged a nervous glance with my mom.

"What do you mean? I need help. Julissa is very good with customers," my mom said. "Okay, we have to go. I have a long drive to Dallas."

I kissed my dad on the cheek and said, "See you next week."

My mom drove me to Tiffani's house, and on the way I asked, "Do you think Dad suspects anything?"

"No, no, he doesn't know," my mom said.

She quickly dropped me off, gave me a kiss, handed me some money, and got on the road to Dallas.

Tiffani's bed had a mattress that pulled out from the bottom, so I had my own space when I spent the night at her house. In the mornings we'd get ready, eat breakfast in her informal dining room, and ride to school together.

Tiffani's house was beautiful. It wasn't a mansion like Clara's, the girl from Spain, but it was much bigger than our apartment, and it was clean and orderly. Tiffani didn't share her bedroom with an office, like I did. My mom kept her fax machine and office supplies in my room.

I loved the time I got to spend at Tiffani's house, but it also made me miss my sisters, especially Nay. I hadn't seen or talked to Nay in months. As difficult as it was with my dad at home, I was still thankful I lived with my parents.

Tiffani's parents were wonderful to me; they welcomed me at their dinner table as if I were Tiffani's sister. I didn't hear them fight at night over money. When I was at Tiffani's house, I felt like a normal American teenage girl.

That Friday, Tiffani's parents picked us up from school, fed us dinner, and took us to the homecoming game. I still felt sad that Tiffani was not on the team with me.

"It's not fair you aren't on the team," I said to Tiffani as we were getting ready in her room.

"It's no big deal. I still get to be part of the pom squad

and go to all the games, even the away ones," she said as she put a ribbon around her ponytail.

We jumped in her dad's truck and went to the football game. I am not sure what came over me, but suddenly I was terrified that my dad knew I was not at the trade show with my mom.

When we got to school, I told Tiffani, "I think my dad knows I am at your house, and he's going to show up at the game and take me away."

"What? No way. He doesn't know you are here. He would have picked you up after school," she said.

Maybe Tiffani was right, but I could not shake the thought from my mind. During the pre-game practice, I was so distracted. But as soon as we went out to the football field and I saw the stands full of students and parents cheering, I let go of the fear.

I joined the other cheerleaders in welcoming the team onto the field.

My dad never showed up that night. A part of me wished he had, so he could support me and feel proud that his daughter was a cheerleader. Instead, after the game Tiffani's parents took us to Fuddruckers, for the "world's greatest hamburgers."

ZOOM ZOOM

WHENEVER MY MOM TOOK JULIO with her to a trade show, my dad and I would spend time at his friend's auto shop. My dad's childhood dream was to own his own mechanic shop. I would say to him, "When I grow up and become rich, I am going to buy you one."

It was at his friend's shop that my dad taught me to listen to the sound of an engine, to detect a pressure leak, to solve a problem with the oil pump, and anything else I needed to know about cars. I would help change the oil on his 1988 Ford, our family truck that had taken us between Mexico and San Antonio many times. We would listen to old José Alfredo Jiménez cassette tapes in my dad's truck, and we bonded over great *ranchera* songs that were such a big part of our heritage. I loved watching my dad in action at the shop. It was his happy place.

Those were good days, *mostly*.

After we finished the oil change one afternoon, I climbed into the truck to do my homework and listen to the radio while my dad played cards and drank beer with his buddies. We'd done that before. He'd have a couple of beers, and then we'd swing by the 7-Eleven near our house. He would buy a six-pack of beer and a Slurpee for me, and then we'd go home to watch *Sábado Gigante*, a popular variety show on Univision.

This day was different, though. He took too long, and it was getting late.

I walked into the shop and found him asleep. I had never seen him that drunk. My dad drank nearly every day, but he was almost methodical about it. He'd drink his beer, crush the can, and then place it on the other side of his living room chair. It seemed as though he was always in control. There were new faces in the shop I had never seen before. I didn't like the way these men looked at me. It made my skin crawl.

"Papi, it's dark outside. I'm hungry," I said, shaking

him awake and guiding him outside to the truck. I said it really loudly so that these men knew he was my dad, and I wasn't alone. We had been in the truck for a few minutes when my dad came to, and demanded to know why he was in the passenger seat.

"You drank too much, Daddy."

"I'm sorry," he said.

He reached into his pocket for the keys, and I reminded him that the truck was already running. "Smart," he said. "Running the radio for that long would have drained the battery if the engine wasn't on."

I smiled because I made him proud. He was too drunk to drive, but the men were making me nervous. I wanted to go home. I sat in the driver's seat for a while before I finally decided it would be best if I drove us home.

Dad taught me to drive around our apartment complex. Surely I can drive us a couple of miles.

I was thirteen.

I leaned over and put his seat belt on. Then I put my seat belt on and adjusted the mirrors. And even though the engine was running, I could hear my heart beating loudly—*pum, pum, pum*. I felt like my heart was going to come out of my body. I backed out of the shop and pulled onto the road just fine. But the farther I drove, the more scared I got.

We reached the first traffic light. It was red. I stopped and watched as cars zoomed by on the crossroad in front of me. I gripped the wheel like my life depended on it. That was when my dad opened his eyes and realized I was driving us home. I thought he would be furious, but he told me to stay calm, and started mumbling instructions as if it were any other driving lesson.

The light turned green, I pressed on the gas, and we made it across safely. Eventually, we made it home. I helped him to his chair in the living room, and he handed me a wad of bills.

"Order some pizza."

QUINCEAÑERA

ARIS GOT MARRIED IN MEXICO toward the end of my eighth-grade year. We all made the trip to Taxco to witness her say "I do." Seeing her dressed in a white ball gown reminded me of how beautiful she had looked in her pink embroidered dress for her *quinceañera*. I still had the Barbie that had stood atop her cake; she had made her way with me to America. My mom had gone to great lengths to find a Barbie with black hair. When Aris turned fifteen, in the 1980s, Barbie dolls of different ethnicities were uncommon.

We didn't stay in Taxco very long. A few months later, I started high school at a small, private, Catholic college-prep school. I had no idea what the next few years would hold. The only thing I looked forward to after three years in the United States was my *quinceañera*. I could vividly picture the church adorned with beautiful red roses, and twirling around for my waltz. I smiled just thinking about it, knowing that it would soon be time for my party. I knew that money was still tight, especially after Aris's wedding, since my parents had used what little money they had saved to pay for it. So I was afraid to bring it up with them. But one day, shortly after my fourteenth birthday, I could not hold it in anymore.

My mom was sitting at the dining room table going over some bills when I said, with a big smile on my face, "Mom, we have to start planning soon."

My mother knew exactly what I was talking about.

I had dreamt about my *quinceañera* since I was three years old, as many Mexican girls do—envisioning a once-in-a-lifetime birthday celebration that would symbolize leaving childhood behind to become a young woman. Pictures and memories from both of my sisters' *quinceañeras* served as constant reminders of how beautiful my big day would be.

"We have time, we have time. We'll talk about it later," my mom said.

I was familiar with my parents' finances; and I knew their tight budget was the reason she didn't want to talk about it. I had watched them work so hard for the last three years, laboring to unbury themselves from the debt of the stolen silver.

Isn't America supposed to be the land of opportunity? Why is money still such a problem?

I tried not to let it bother me. I was sure my mom would figure something out. She always had a solution. She had promised me a party like Aris's, and she always kept her promises, except for the time she missed *La Escolta*, but that was a long time ago. I trusted we would start planning soon enough.

In order to ease my mom's concern over the money the party would cost, I got on the phone to discuss it with some of my family in Mexico, without either of my parents knowing.

One afternoon, when I was home alone with Julio, I dialed Mama Silvia's house.

"*Hola, Mama Silvia,*" I said as soon as she picked up.

"Natzely? How are you?" my grandma asked, sounding surprised that I was calling her.

"Mama Silvia, I am going to be fifteen next year, and

I really want to have my party in Mexico. But you know how my parents are still struggling, so I was wondering if you could help pitch in for my party?"

"Of course, *mija*. I can help pay for the food. Call your *tias* and ask them to be your *madrinas* for the cake and the music," she said.

After we got off the phone, I called my aunts, and asked them to be my godmothers, as my grandma had suggested. One agreed to be the sponsor for the cake, the other for the music, and Tio Alex agreed to pay for the food. Tio Mike agreed to pay for the rest of the expenses. I imagined how pleased my parents would be when they found out I'd figured a way to help save them money for my party.

The weeks went by and my mother never brought it up. So the moment she walked in the door after one of her trips, I started talking about my plans.

"So, I've been thinking. I really want to have my *quinceañera* in Mexico, since that's where all our family is. Maybe even at Hotel de la Borda, like Aris's, since it's so beautiful there. And—"

"I am tired, not right now, okay," she said. "You know we don't have that kind of money."

"I know, but I was thinking that Uncle Mike and Mama Silvia could help."

"Your grandmother and uncle already help with your sisters," she said.

"I called them and they said they would help."

Dad sighed. "Ay, *mija*."

My mother closed her eyes and pressed the palms of her hands against them. She looked so sad. I regretted saying anything at all.

"I promise we can do this without spending a lot of money," I said.

"Your mother said she doesn't want to talk about this right now," my dad said.

"I'm willing to help," I pleaded. "And I know the whole family will help. I just know it. My dress doesn't have to be—"

"You can't go back to Mexico," my mother said as she pulled her hands away from her eyes and looked right into my own.

"What do you mean?" I asked.

"If you go to Mexico, you will never be able to come back to the US."

I didn't understand.

"But I went to Aris's wedding last summer," I said.

"Your visa is expired now. You can't go back to Mexico, and you cannot have a *quinceañera*."

"But why?!" I screamed. I could not believe my ears.

I knew I didn't have a social security number, but my mom had said I had a visa, and now it was expired. So without it, how would I be able to stay in school? I quickly dismissed the thought, since not having a *quinceañera* was all I would think about that night.

"I am sorry, but there is nothing we can do. You cannot have a *quinceañera*. I am so sorry."

"I hate you!" I screamed. "I hate it here!"

"Julissa, sit down!" my dad yelled.

I stormed into my bedroom, yelling, "Why did you ever bring me here!" And I slammed the door. I'd been looking forward to my *quinceañera* for as long as I could remember. And now they had taken that away from me too.

UNDOCUMENTED

THE NEXT NIGHT AS I lay in bed, a whole new series of questions and thoughts entered my mind: *Why could I never visit Mexico again? And if I did, was it true that I could never come back to America?*

All I'd heard was that I couldn't have a *quinceañera*, and I knew this wasn't a party that I could throw for myself when I was older. It wasn't a moment I could re-create. It would be gone forever.

I was too young, or maybe too naïve, to understand that on that night my mother had shared a secret that would define and haunt me for years to come. The consequences were much greater than not having a party. My family was in Mexico, but my parents were here. My life was in both places. There had to be some way around it. What if Tiffani's parents could adopt me? I figured that would make me an official American citizen. Certainly that would take care of my visa problem. I started to think about my expired visa as a problem I could fix.

I had told Tiffani about my devastating news. She didn't even need to say anything. I could see how much she cared for me. She had become more like a sister than a friend. My own sisters felt like they were a million miles away. I hardly spoke to them, especially now that Aris was married.

I spoke to Tiffani's parents the next time I saw them, and they agreed to adopt me if my parents allowed it. That was how much they loved me. But my parents were too proud to have their daughter adopted, even if it was just to gain my American citizenship.

My parents didn't have any other solutions for my expired visa. I don't think they realized what being undocumented would mean for my future. And yet, *I* started to figure out what it meant pretty quickly.

I was in my parents' room watching TV one morning when I came across Fox News. I stopped on the channel because the anchor, a beautiful blond woman, was talking about Mexican immigrants living in Texas. I was a Mexican immigrant living in Texas. I watched the report in horror as the TV host called Mexican immigrants without legal status, or citizenship, "illegals" and "illegal aliens." I was smart enough to know that as a fourteen-year-old high school freshman, I was now one of them.

I was no longer just "a Mexican," which seemed bad enough in certain people's eyes. I was an "illegal," or worse, an "illegal alien"—like some thing from another planet that wasn't even human. The news reported on the "illegals" the way they would report on a murderer or a thief. But I was just a girl worried about not having a pretty pink dress.

My face got hot with anger. I wanted to jump in the TV and yell, "I am not an alien!" When I thought about criminals, I didn't picture someone like me. I imagined a person who robbed, stole, or killed. Yet people seemed to throw the word *illegal* around with the same disgust in their voice.

Is that how people would treat me if they knew?

I didn't feel illegal. I didn't think anyone suspected

anything. Having an expired visa didn't make me feel like a criminal. I moved seamlessly from middle school to high school, just like any other student. I had good grades, and my accent was almost gone, so no one questioned anything—and it quickly became clear that's the way it had to stay.

"You can't tell anyone," my mom told me. "If anyone finds out, you could be deported."

Deportation meant I would be separated from my parents and my little brother. I would have a criminal record in the United States. I could end up in a detention center, a kind of jail for men, women, and children who are undocumented. Making sure I never said anything about my visa or my status became front and center in every conversation I had from that moment forward. I didn't want to be deported. I didn't want to be separated from my parents. As bad as things were sometimes, they were my parents, and I loved them. America was my home now.

Soon my own parents started using my immigration status as a threat: "Don't you go breaking any laws, Julissa. You'll get deported." When I was little, they used to threaten me with La Llorona, the Mexican female version of the boogeyman. As I got older I realized the Llorona wasn't real, but the *Migra*, or ICE (Immigration and Customs Enforcement), wasn't something mythical to scare children. The *Migra* was real, and scarier than any monster I could imagine.

BETRAYAL

MY MOM TOOK ME ALONG to one of her trade shows that was far enough away that we had to fly. We could bring four carry-ons filled with silver. Sam didn't go on this trip, but he did help us pack, and took care of our itineraries. This was a big show, and we brought a lot more silver than usual, which meant we had to check one large bag of jewelry to go under the plane.

Once we landed back home in San Antonio, we got off the plane and made it to the baggage area. Everyone's luggage was already going around on the conveyor belt. We waited as everyone else grabbed their bags and left, but our luggage—the large bag full of thousands of dollars' worth of silver—never showed up. My mother was in a panic. She was pacing back and forth, and the color drained from her face.

"Mom, are you okay?"

"Yes, yes, I am okay," she said.

"Maybe you should sit down," I said, noticing that she looked faint. "Mom, do you think it's a coincidence that our bag of silver disappeared? Someone had to know to pick up *that* bag."

The airline was positive the bag came off the plane. It wasn't lost. It wasn't sent to another airport by mistake.

"Mom, the only other person who knew when we were landing was Sam," I said.

My mother stared at me in complete disbelief. "No. He would never do that."

I insisted I knew this wasn't a mistake. Someone didn't just take the bag by accident.

When my dad showed up to pick us up, he couldn't believe it. He was furious. Not at my mom, or at me, but at life.

"Why does this always happen to us?" he said out loud.

My mom didn't want to call the cops. I would have to

help her translate, and she was afraid they would ask to see my ID or ask about my immigration status.

"But, Mom, we didn't do anything wrong," I explained.

Eventually we filed a report with the police, and their investigation led them to Sam's place, in our same apartment complex. After the cops went to Sam's, he came to beg my mom and dad not to press charges.

My dad opened the door, but he didn't let Sam inside.

"Julio, please don't press charges. Please, I will pay you back. I am so sorry," he said, crying.

He handed a small box of jewelry to my dad. He had sold most of what he'd stolen for little money.

My dad took the box and closed the door without saying a word.

My mom refused to press charges. He was a friend, she said. "A *trusted* friend."

She insisted she couldn't do that to him. "I can't imagine him in jail."

Slowly, it dawned on my parents that Sam had been stealing from them for years. He knew their travel routines, and everything else about them. It was likely that he was responsible for the robbery when they stopped at the diner in Laredo a few years back. It wasn't like someone threw a brick through the van window and grabbed a few pieces. They cut that window out and made off with every single box. It *had* to have been Sam's doing. I started to wonder how much silver had disappeared over the years. I was furious that my mother just let him get away with it, but at the same time I was taken by her compassion and ability to forgive.

Sometimes when I look at old pictures of Sam with my family, I want to tear those pictures apart. Did he consider for one second the hardship he put us through? Did he know how much stress he caused? Did he think about what he had done to all of us? To me? Sam had been like an uncle to me. He watched over Julio and me when my parents were away. Whenever I was upset with my dad, I would turn to Sam. He didn't just hurt my parents; he also betrayed me.

Sam deserved to go to jail, and it stung every time my father's stress bubbled to the surface in a fit of rage. My dad's temper and drinking got worse. Even though he tried to stop drinking, he couldn't. He was an alcoholic. My mom staged an intervention with the pastor from our church. He came to our house, spoke to my dad, and tried to offer help. But alcoholism is a disease, and without proper treatment, he always went back to drinking.

He started screaming louder and hitting harder. I swore to myself I wasn't going to take it anymore. I started threatening my dad, "If you hit me, I am going to call 911!" But I used the police in the same way my parents used La Llorona. It was an empty threat. He was my father and I loved him unconditionally, despite his disease.

NEW BEGINNINGS

ONE WEEKEND WHILE I WAS doing laundry, Sam was too. When he walked into the communal laundry room, his eyes grew bigger than usual through his thick glasses at the sight of me. Sam stood at the door with his laundry basket, deciding if he should come in.

Before he could decide, I said, "You can't come in here. Thieves are not allowed in the laundry room." His whole head turned red. Sam stood at the doorway for a second and then turned around and left. My heart was pounding, and as soon as he left, I started sobbing. I threw the clothes into the basket and waited until Sam was out of sight before making my way back to our apartment.

When I got home, I said to my dad, "I saw Sam at the laundry room and told him thieves were not allowed to come in."

"You shouldn't have said anything. He doesn't even deserve us looking at him."

"I don't know why we still live here! We are going to keep running into him."

"I know. I already told your mom we need to move."

A couple of weeks later, my dad ran into Sam in the parking lot. Every time we saw him walking around freely, it felt like salt on an open wound. I kept asking my parents to move far from Sam—and they finally agreed.

The new house wasn't fancy, but it had a yard and three bedrooms, and was located in a nice neighborhood far away from Sam.

After Sam's theft at the airport, my mom stopped going to trade shows, because she couldn't get another loan to buy more jewelry. Sam's actions didn't just force us to live in a different part of town, they also meant my mom needed a new way to support our family.

Instead of going to the trade shows, my parents started selling the remaining silver at fairs and festivals. But they didn't earn enough money from the festivals.

"What are we going to do now?" I asked my mom one afternoon after opening the mail and finding an angry letter from our landlord because we were late on the rent.

"Don't worry, *mija*. Money is not really a problem, because you can always work harder to make more of it. We'll find a way," she said.

My mom saw the volume of funnel cakes that were sold during our trips to Six Flags and decided to start selling them at the festivals too. One weekend, my mom and I got in the car and drove to the restaurant supply district in San Antonio.

"Mom, how did you find this place?" I asked when we arrived at a huge parking lot with warehouses surrounding us.

"I asked around until someone told me where I could buy a fryolator," she said.

I've always been so impressed by my mom's ability to find solutions. This was before Google, and she didn't speak English fluently, but somehow she figured it out. We didn't have enough money to buy a real food truck, the kind that are so popular and trendy these days, so we only bought a fryolator. We would load it into the back of my dad's pickup truck for every festival. Later, my mom would also purchase a roasted-corn machine. Dough and corn were inexpensive to purchase, which meant we made a good profit from every funnel cake and roasted corn we sold, but we had to sell a lot of them to make any real money. That meant long hours, greasy-smelling clothes, and occasional burns from the oil in the fryolator. But none of that stopped my parents. I never heard my mom complain once.

"Mom, you work so much. Don't you get tired?" I asked her.

"I am grateful. A lot of people don't have a job," she said.

I hated seeing how hard she labored, and sometimes she made little money from the festivals. But the one silver lining of Sam's betrayal was that my mom spent more time in San Antonio.

During the week, after school, I helped my mom at Fort Sam Houston, a military base that had a mall, called the PX, where we sold silver jewelry. On the weekends, we worked at the Market Square, an open market in San Antonio, where we sold funnel cakes, smoothies, tacos, and anything else we could cook.

My parents' priority was to provide for us and to put

us on a path for success. As long as they were earning an honest living, they would do any job necessary. My mom didn't care if she was a stereotype—a Mexican woman selling tacos—because she was providing for her family, and that was what mattered.

During one of my rare phone calls with Nay, she said, "Everyone thinks you all should come back to Taxco. What's mom doing selling *tacos*?"

"Everyone doesn't know how hard mom works to pay for everything," I said.

"Mom doesn't pay for everything. Mama Silvia pays for my tuition," Nay complained.

My family in Mexico was gossiping about it like it was a bad thing: "Luisa is now selling *tacos*." As if it was some kind of failure. It didn't bother my mom. That's one of the many things I love about my parents. They were hard workers, and no honest work was beneath them.

THE SAN ANTONIO SPURS

ONE THING I TRULY LOVED about San Antonio was how the whole city rallied behind our NBA team, the Spurs. It made it easy to fall in love with the team.

I couldn't talk with my friends about many pop culture references. I wasn't allowed to watch MTV. But I could speak about Avery Johnson, Sean Elliott, Tim Duncan, and "The Admiral" David Robinson. My love for sports always made me feel like I belonged in America.

During the 1999 championship season my parents splurged a little and let me take Julio to a Spurs game. We weren't rolling in money, but after we started selling funnel cakes, things improved.

My dad dropped Julio and me off a few blocks from the Alamodome, the arena where the Spurs played at the time.

"I'll pick you up at this same spot when the game is over. Have fun," he said.

I put all the negotiation skills I'd learned from my mom into practice and got a great deal on a pair of tickets. Seated in a stadium, surrounded by thousands of Spurs fans, I could forget about being "illegal." I was just a normal American kid who loved sports.

When we got to our seats, I realized we were three rows from the floor.

"Wow! These are our seats?" Julio asked in disbelief.

"I know! I can't believe it!"

We were sitting next to a family of four. They looked like the white version of our family. Julio noticed and said, "I wish Mom and Dad could've come with us."

But we could only afford two tickets.

The Spurs were playing the Portland Trail Blazers, and so far the game was pretty terrible. We were down by eighteen points going into the third quarter.

"Why did we even come? This game sucks," Julio said.

"Well, we didn't know they were going to lose. But there is time, we can still win."

"How? We are down by eighteen points!"

Then the Spurs went on a run and began catching up.

Each time the Spurs scored, Julio and I high-fived each other and the people around us. The mom seated next to me said, "Your son is so cute."

"He's my brother."

Julio was seven years old, but he was really tall for his age. He looked like he could have been nine years old.

How can she think he's my son!

I really wished my parents had come to the game with us.

The game got really exciting, but I stopped giving high fives to the mom.

With twelve seconds left in the game, and the Spurs down two points, Sean Elliott scored a three-pointer while barely staying inbounds. We won by one point! The Alamodome went crazy. Everyone jumped out of their seats and began chanting, "Go, Spurs, go!" At one point, Julio got so excited that he took off his favorite David Robinson jersey and started swinging it over his head.

Somehow, in the crowd, his jersey got lost. He started crying at the top of his lungs.

"Don't cry, Julio, we just won an amazing game."

"But my jersey, I want my jersey," he said, in between sobs.

When the game was over, we stayed behind to look for his jersey as everyone else filtered out of the stadium. An usher saw Julio crying and asked what was wrong.

"My little brother lost his favorite David Robinson jersey," I explained.

"Oh no! Come with me."

The usher gave us a brand-new shirt and then took us down to the locker room. We waited outside for over an hour for the players to shower and leave the locker room. The whole time I was thinking, *Dad is going to be so mad. He's probably worried about us. I'll never go to another Spurs game again.*

Finally David Robinson, Sean Elliott, and Tim Duncan came out of the locker room and gave us high fives. David Robinson even signed Julio's shirt. We didn't get to take pictures with the players, since cell phones with cameras didn't exist yet. But I'll always remember that day.

When we finally got outside to my dad's car, he was really upset.

"I'm so sorry, but look," I said, showing him my brother's newly signed T-shirt. Then my dad became just as excited as Julio and me; everyone in San Antonio loves the Spurs.

NOT FOR ME

LIFE AT SCHOOL WAS MISERABLE. I'd hoped the bullying in middle school wouldn't follow me to high school, but I was wrong. In middle school, girls made fun of my lunch or my long hair. Now I was surrounded by a group of girls who had nothing better to do than call me fat. One day I was in the locker room changing into my shorts and T-shirt for gym class. As I took off my shirt, a girl standing next to me started laughing.

"Why are you laughing?" I asked.

I wasn't the same quiet girl who once let people make fun of her. I spoke English now, and I stood up for myself.

"Your roll!" she said.

"They are called curves. Sorry you don't have any," I said, closed my locker, and ran into the bathroom.

It was one more reason why private school was not for me.

I think my mom had this idea that if I went to public school I wouldn't get a good education or that I would get into trouble. But the public high school I would have attended was a great school; they offered more college-level classes than my private college-prep high school.

Later in the school year, a pretty blond girl named Amy transferred into our sophomore class. In our health class she made a presentation about eating disorders and how dangerous they were. She said, "Bullying contributed to my eating disorder. Please be nice to each other."

After class, I went up to her and said, "Amy, thank you for sharing. I am really sorry you had to go through that."

"Thanks, Julissa. That's really nice of you."

I was really nice to her, thinking she could probably

use a friend. A few weeks later when class let out, I saw her in the hall by the lockers. I went up to her and said hello.

"Eww, I don't talk to fat girls," she said.

All the snooty girls around us laughed.

I shot back, "Excuse me. I may be fat, but at least I'm happy."

I didn't feel fat, but I wanted her to know that even if she thought I was fat, I was happy with the way I looked.

"I've got to get out of this school," I begged my mom almost every day.

I would also say to her, "You struggle to pay my tuition. Public school would be so much better, please, Mom."

My education and getting ahead in life were way more important to her than the money it cost. Eventually, though, my mom saw how unhappy I was and agreed to enroll me in public school. It turned out that I didn't need a social security number to enroll in school.

I decided to start things off on the right foot at Theodore Roosevelt High School. Instead of trying to fit in, I decided to be myself. That summer I auditioned for the school dance team. This time I knew what to wear—not like during my middle school audition for the cheerleading squad when I wore shorts and a T-shirt.

I made it, and when I met all the girls from the team before school started, they immediately embraced me. I could tell right away this experience was going to be different from Catholic school.

From the first day it was obvious that it wasn't just a school full of rich kids. There were people who rode the bus to school, and there were also a few superfancy cars parked in the student parking lot. There were students of every race and ethnicity too. I felt at home. Instantly. I was blown away by the public school experience.

☆

The first time I saw Chris I was with my dance-team girls in the cafeteria, a couple of weeks before school started. We had just finished practice, and he was walking from the administrative office. He was half-white and half-Black, and he had this curly hair that was frosted yellow on top. He was wearing a red mesh backpack. I leaned over to ask my friend Latoya, "Who is that?"

She said, "Girl, everybody likes Chris."

He'll never like me was the only thought that crossed my mind.

About ten minutes into my history class on that very first day of school, a student walked in late. I looked up and saw it was Chris—my heart started beating fast.

There were a bunch of seats open in the classroom, yet he came and sat down at the desk right in front of mine. At that moment, I was positive that going to public school was the best thing that had ever happened to me.

Chris was on the baseball team, and he was funny. People really liked him. I really liked him. My parents didn't allow me to date, so I spent time getting to know Chris over phone calls and at school. At night, I would sneak the phone into my room so I could talk to him. Because our phone was in the kitchen, I had to wait until my parents were asleep, then run the cord out the sliding door into the backyard, all the way around the house, and in through my bedroom window. Julio and I shared a room, and he never told on me when I did that. Not once.

One night while I was talking to Chris, my dad heard me laughing and tried to open the door to our room.

I had locked the door.

"Open the door!" he yelled, his voice rising in anger.

That's when Julio opened the door. I hung up the phone without saying good-bye.

"Who are you talking to?" my dad asked.

"She's telling me jokes," Julio said.

"Oh," my dad said. "All right, then...."

I will owe Julio for that one forever.

I wanted to open up to Chris about my past, and my uncertain present. He had confided in me about his mom's cancer and his dad's past, so I wanted to tell him that I was undocumented and how afraid I was every day that someone might find out. I was afraid to be deported and separated from my family. But I kept hearing my mother's words over again: "You can't tell anyone."

One time, Chris invited me to meet him at a friend's party on a Friday night. I wanted to go, but I knew my parents wouldn't let me. As the school day went on, I became angry, thinking about how strict my parents were. I wasn't even allowed to go to the movies with friends. I felt as if I were imprisoned in a cage. I needed to break free.

My dad picked me up every day after dance practice. I knew he would show up and I wouldn't be there. I was so nervous thinking about how angry he was going to be. I knew disobeying my parents was wrong, but I also felt it was so unfair that they never let me go anywhere.

I skipped dance practice and left with a friend. When I got to my friend's house I called my mom. I didn't want her to worry. But it was too late.

"Your dad is going crazy. He was so worried about you. He couldn't find you at school, and you didn't go to dance practice. What is wrong with you?" my mom asked angrily on the phone.

I told her I was okay, and I would come home after the party.

"No, you're not going. Where are you?" she asked in her sternest voice. "Give me the address. We're coming to pick you up."

I didn't tell my mom where I was. I just said that I wasn't running away and that I really wanted to go to the party. Then I hung up.

My parents had caller ID on their phone, which

I didn't think about, so they kept calling back. My friend and I just unplugged the phone. By that time there were a couple of other friends with us. They were concerned.

"Are you sure? Are you sure this is okay?" they repeatedly asked me.

I knew it wasn't okay, but I said, "Yes, it's fine."

By the time we walked into the house where the party was being held, there were tons of people there—including Chris. He lit up with a big smile as soon as he saw me. I had never been someone who was invited to the parties at any of my other schools. Now I was invited to all the parties, and for the first time, I was actually at one.

Chris and I started dancing, and I just felt on top of the world. All thoughts of my immigration status, my dad's anger, and the mean girls at my old school left my mind.

And then, right in the middle of it, the cops showed up.

Somebody stopped the music and yelled, "Run!" All of a sudden, everyone scattered. Chris and I ran through the backyard until we reached a fence, hopped over, and turned down an alley. No one was chasing us, so we slowed down, but I was in a panic. Chris didn't understand why I was so worried. "The worst thing that could happen is they might call your parents or you might get a ticket," he said.

I'm going to go to jail and I'm going to get deported and my life is going to be over.

I never told Chris about my fear. I just said, "I cannot get a ticket."

Ever since my mom had told me I was undocumented two years before, I had spent every minute being conscious of every single thing I did and said, so that no one would learn I was in the country illegally. I felt stressed all the time. Any wrong move could be the one that got me thrown out of the country. And my parents never let me forget it.

Chris managed to find us a ride, and as I rode in the car with him, I made up my mind that there were going to be times when I just had to live. And in those moments, I knew: If I got caught, then I got caught. I couldn't imagine living my entire life in a cage. If I didn't take a risk, I wouldn't feel alive.

I can't remember if my dad hit me that night or if I got grounded.

On Monday morning at school, I went to my locker to drop off my books and I found a perfectly folded note from Chris: *I want to be with you.*

REUNITED

ARIS HAD BEEN MARRIED FOR a couple of years when she moved to San Antonio with her husband, Victor. They moved in with us while they saved money to get their own place. For a while my dad didn't drink, didn't yell, and didn't hit me. I think he wanted to be on his best behavior around my sister and her husband.

After Aris had been living with us for a few weeks, I confessed I had a boyfriend and told her all about Chris. We were in the living room one afternoon while my dad and Victor worked on the truck outside.

"We've been dating for a couple of months, but I hate that I can't even go to the movies with him," I told her.

"Dad is way too strict. He never let me have a boy-friend either. I would never have married Victor if Dad lived in Mexico," she joked.

I had never been very close to Aris when I was a young girl in Mexico; our ten-year age difference made us have little in common. But now that I was a teenager, I could confide in my sister, and she was more than happy to listen and help.

My friends at school knew that I wasn't allowed to have a boyfriend, and they wanted to help me have a date with Chris. The plan was to convince my dad to let me go to the movies. They would all come but see a different film so Chris and I could be alone. Aris was the mastermind behind the plan, and she would drive me.

One Friday night, I begged my dad to let me go to the movies. I wasn't sure the plan would work.

"Dad, don't be so mean. Let her go. I'll drive her," Aris jumped in.

"Fine, but only this time."

I couldn't believe my dad was letting me go to the movies. Aris drove me to the theater and said she would pick me up at 10:00 PM, an hour after the movie ended.

"We can drop Chris off after the movie. I want to meet him," she said.

"Thank you so much, Aris. I love you."

My girlfriends left after the movie. Chris and I walked to the arcade next door and waited for Aris to pick us up. At 10:00 PM sharp, I saw my parents' black SUV coming through the parking lot. My dad was driving.

I let go of Chris's hand and immediately started feeling something like a warm liquid coming down my neck and into my shoulders. It was fear.

"Are you okay?" he asked.

"My dad didn't know I was coming to the movies with you. He is going to be so mad."

My dad didn't pull up to the curb. He drove past us, made a left turn, and continued through the parking lot. A minute later, I saw my mom and Aris walking toward us.

"Why is Dad here?" I asked Aris.

"He knew something was up. He refused to let me pick you up."

I turned to Mom. "I am sorry. He was never going to let me come."

Chris just stood next to me, not saying a word. My mom turned to him and said, "Sorry, we can't take you home," and handed me a twenty-dollar bill.

"Tell him he is going to need to take a taxi home. Your dad isn't going to drive him."

I turned to Chris and translated what my mom had told me. "I am so sorry. I am so embarrassed," I said.

"Don't be. I just hope you are not in a lot of trouble. I'll see you at school on Monday," he said and leaned in for a hug. I pulled away; I knew my dad was probably watching from the parking lot.

My mom led the way. I looked at Aris and shook my head.

"I am sorry, Juli," she said.

"It's okay. You were just trying to help."

I got in the backseat. My dad didn't say a word to me, but when we got home he pulled out his belt.

CASH MONEY

I DATED CHRIS FOR A few months, until he moved away. The holidays during my junior year in high school had me feeling left behind.

It had been years since my mom had spent the holidays in Mexico with Mama Silvia and the rest of our family. I couldn't go back because of my expired visa, and I needed to stay behind with my dad and work the funnel cake stand on New Year's Eve—a potentially huge moneymaking night with all the festivities happening in San Antonio, and a night we simply couldn't afford to miss. Aris and her husband also joined my mom in Mexico, since their visas were not expired.

My dad was tense heading into New Year's Eve.

"We paid so much money for this permit. We have to sell a lot of funnel cakes to break even," he said as we were unloading the pickup truck.

"There are a lot of people already here; we'll sell a lot of funnel cakes," I said, trying to cheer him up.

Business started really slowly. There were a lot of people at the plaza where we were set up, but none of them were buying funnel cakes. My dad was pacing back and forth behind the fryolator. I could sense his worry.

Then, almost like magic, customers started lining up for funnel cakes.

I quickly went from being afraid of not making enough money to being scared my dad would blow up because the line was too long and we weren't keeping up. We desperately needed more help. There was no way the two of us could handle the crowd. But it was too late. There was no one we could call. People in line started shouting at us: "What's the holdup?" "Come on!"

I ran back and forth from the fryolator to the counter, wiping sweat from my forehead, spilling powdered sugar everywhere, making greasy, floppy messes of the dollar bills I handed back as change.

That's when I noticed a familiar face in the line: Tiffani! I hadn't seen her since I'd switched schools, but she smiled, started waving at me, and pushed her way to the front. "You look like you need help," she said.

"Hi! Yeah, we can't keep up," I said, turning away quickly to flip the funnel cakes in the fryer before they burned.

"I'll be right back," Tiffani said, and off she went. I saw her talking to her dad and then making her way back toward the stand, pulling her hair up into a ponytail as she elbowed her way through the crowd.

All of a sudden she walked right into the stand with us.

"Okay," she said. "I'll put the powdered sugar on the funnel cakes and charge people. Julissa, you make the funnel cakes, and, Julio, you make the mix."

I looked up at my dad, worried to death that he would be upset that Tiffani had come barging in, ordering us around, but to my surprise, he welcomed the help. "Okay," Dad said with a big smile. "Thank you."

I wanted to hug her, but the line was too long to stop.

Tiffani spent the next three hours with us, knee-deep in customers and suffering from the heat of the fryolators. We fell into a rhythm like a well-oiled—or, at least, a well-greased—machine. With Tiffani's help, I was sure we'd sold far more funnel cakes in a single night than we'd ever sold before, even with Mom.

At the stroke of midnight, Tiffani grabbed a fistful of powdered sugar and threw it up in the air. "Happy New Year!" she exclaimed. My dad laughed and gave her a hug.

Shortly after midnight, Tiffani's dad came by to pick her up.

"Thank you, thank you. I love you. Thank you!" I said to them.

"You know it. And don't be a stranger; call me sometime," she said.

It felt good to see the two of them and to reconnect at the start of a brand-new year. There simply weren't enough words to express my gratitude, and my father thanked them too.

Once again, Tiffani was my savior. She would always be my American sister.

It took my dad and me two hours to clean up that night before we loaded the truck and drove home, and my dad seemed happy the whole time.

Once we were home, the two of us were far too wired to go to sleep. We were excited about counting the day's spoils.

My dad sat on a chair and gave me a nervous smile as I neatly laid out rows of one-, five-, ten-, and twenty-dollar bills on the bed. I was still wearing the same clothes and smelled of powdered sugar, funnel cake mix, and grease—but the smell of those green bills overpowered everything.

"I don't think we've ever made so many funnel cakes in one night."

"No," my dad said. He seemed happy. Calm. I hadn't seen him like that in a very long time.

I usually had a pretty good idea of what we made on any given day, but at five dollars for a small funnel cake, six dollars for a large one, and two dollars extra for strawberries, I had completely lost track that night, and counting those bills gave me quite a shock.

"How much?" my dad said.

"Hold on. I have to count again," I told him.

The anticipation was killing him, I could tell. He seemed like a kid waiting to open his Christmas presents.

After I finished counting for the fifth time, I finally asked him, "Guess how much money we made?"

"How much?"

"Come on. Guess!"

"A million dollars?" he said slowly, with a smile.

"Close," I said. "Ten thousand dollars!"

My dad's eyes got really big. He stood up. He grabbed a pile of bills and threw them in the air.

"We're rich!" he yelled. He laughed. My father was laughing!

"Ha-haaaaa!" he yelled, jumping up on the bed full of money and holding out his hand for me to join him.

I got on the bed and jumped up and down with him. We threw bills up in the air and watched them fall to the bed while yelling, "*¡Somos ricos! ¡Somos ricos!*" Of course, we weren't rich, but it felt that way that night.

It was such a rare moment of joy with my dad that I threw myself into it like I had when I was a little girl.

If money was what made my dad smile and my mom spend more time with her family, then I was determined to do well in school, go to college, and get an amazing job that paid me lots of money.

REGRET

NIGHTS FULL OF LAUGHTER BETWEEN my dad and me were faint memories that I would often cling to. I wished and prayed that my dad would get better, that he would seek treatment for his disease, and that he would be a good father all the time. But my prayers weren't answered.

Aris and her husband had moved out of our house and into their own apartment. One night, shortly after my sister left, my dad lost it. I don't remember what made him angry, but instead of directing his rage toward me, he directed it at my mom.

We were in the living room when I saw him push my mom and then slap her on the arm.

"Stop it, Dad!" I yelled.

"It's okay, *mija*. Go to your room," my mom yelled as she moved away from my dad.

Julio was already sleeping, and I was glad he was not seeing my dad like this. My dad moved closer to my mom and grabbed her hair, yanking her like she was a rag doll.

"I am going to call 911 if you don't stop," I yelled at him.

But he was in such a fury he didn't even hear me. Julio woke up from all the noise.

"Papi, let her go!" Julio screamed in horror as he ran to my mom's aid. I grabbed his shirt and stopped him before he could reach my parents.

"Do something!" Julio said, looking at me with tears in his eyes.

I picked up the phone.

"No! Don't, Julissa!" my mom yelled. "What if they ask to see your ID? What if they ask questions? You could get in trouble!" My dad was still holding her by her hair.

The fear of my mom getting hurt was stronger than my fear of getting deported.

"Dad, let her go!" I said again, but by now he had dragged her to the kitchen.

I didn't want to dial 911, but I punched the numbers on the phone anyway. It was almost like an out-of-body experience.

"911, what's your emergency?"

I thought about hanging up, but even after seeing me dial, my dad didn't let go of Mom.

"911, what's your emergency?" The operator repeated.

"My dad is drunk and hitting my mom." I kept a cool, calm voice that surprised even me. Julio was crying in the background.

"Get to a safe place. The police are on their way."

My bedroom had become my safe place. But I wasn't going to hide and abandon my mom. By the time two policemen knocked on our door, my dad had calmed down.

I opened the door and the cops walked into the house. My dad was sitting on the couch. They pulled him up and took him away in handcuffs. He didn't resist. My dad stared at the floor, keeping his eyes from looking at me. He looked defeated, broken, and I felt like it was all my fault.

I regretted calling the police the moment I laid eyes on them, and I'll regret it forever.

How could I have called the police on my own dad?

It was the first time I understood that for undocumented immigrants, every single decision has potentially life-altering consequences. Nothing is ever simple. There would always be more consequences to face. I did the right thing by calling the police, but I had also done a terrible thing, and the fallout would be earth-shattering.

My dad was in jail for one night. When he came back home, he apologized.

Under normal circumstances, our relationship might have improved after that night. The threat of going to prison, an arrest record, and the shame of going to jail might have been what my dad needed to turn his life around. But our situation was anything but normal.

What I didn't know when I called the police was that he would be deported. He had a valid visa, but for legal reasons I didn't understand, he was forced to leave the country for six months.

"I am sorry," I said before he left.

He didn't say anything back.

With one phone call, I turned my mom into a single parent. I hardly remember what those six months were like without him, except for the fact that everything was harder. My dad was the one who drove Julio and me to school. He picked us up, cooked us dinner, and took me to my basketball games and dance practices. My mom did the best she could to make up for his absence, but she wasn't as organized. The house was a constant mess, and I was late to every practice. I didn't have to deal with my dad's anger and drinking, but that didn't mean I didn't miss and need my dad. I wish I didn't grow up feeling afraid of him. But I also thought if he was mean all the time, then hating him wouldn't hurt so much.

The stress also brought out another side of my mom. One day, Julio and I were playing in the living room, and he hit me really hard with his toy sword. I hit him back and he started crying. My mom ran over and hit me. I couldn't believe it.

I decided to spend as much time as I could away from home. School became a sanctuary for me. I buried myself in my studies and activities, knowing that they were my way out of this situation. I read about colleges all over the country, in faraway places. Even though I was undocumented, I still believed in the American Dream—if I worked hard enough and earned good grades, I believed I could get into college and leave all this sadness and craziness behind.

THE COLLEGE DREAM

MY DAD WAS BACK AFTER six months in Mexico. We never spoke about what happened that night, and everything went back to the way it was before. In early September of my senior year, I walked into my school's college counselor office. I went to a big public school, so each counselor was responsible for hundreds of students. She asked for my name, even though I had been to her office several times. She turned to her computer and began typing. A couple of minutes later she said, "You have excellent grades and great extracurricular activities, and I am sure your teachers will write you very compelling letters of recommendation."

I smiled, feeling proud of my accomplishments. Then she told me I still needed to take the SAT, a college admissions test. My parents didn't attend college, so I didn't have guidance about the application process at home.

"You can apply to any college or university; none of them are out of reach," the counselor added. "Do you have any questions?"

I wanted to ask her if being undocumented would be a problem, but I was embarrassed and scared to reveal my immigration status to her.

She doesn't even know my name. I can't trust her.

"No. Thank you," I said nervously, looking down at my feet.

I left her office feeling hopeful. I was ready to escape, but going to college was about more than just leaving an unhappy home. It was the next step in my American Dream. I imagined what it would feel like to be important, successful, and powerful.

I wanted to make money so I could solve all our problems. I would finish building my parents' dream home in Mexico, send my dad to a rehabilitation center, and pay for Julio's education. I would resolve my immigration status so I wouldn't have to be afraid of getting deported, and I would rise above all the challenges my family and I faced to live the great promise that America gives to so many.

If I were rich and successful, why would anyone turn me away?

A few weeks later my dad drove me to school on a Saturday morning to take the SAT. I had taken a few practice tests, but I still felt unprepared. I hadn't taken any preparation classes because I didn't learn about them in time, and more important, we couldn't afford them. But when I received my score, I was surprised to see that I did better than I expected.

Every evening after school, after helping my mom sell silver jewelry at Fort Sam Houston, and when my homework was done, I would work on my college applications.

"You work too hard, and you might not even be able to go," my dad said one evening.

My mom overheard him. "That's not true. *Mija*, you work as hard as you can. If you work hard, and stay out of trouble, anything is possible in this country," she said.

"I know, Mom, I know."

I applied to more than a dozen colleges over the course of two weeks. Then I waited. I was very hopeful that by

October I would have a good idea of what area of the country I would move to. I checked the mail every day, and then finally the first letter arrived from Georgetown University.

We regret to inform you...

I was so disappointed, but Georgetown was a very prestigious university, where students like me with straight As, college prep classes, and glowing recommendations sometimes didn't get in.

I waited for more letters to arrive, but each one said the same thing: *We regret to inform you...*

After receiving a rejection letter from Colorado College, I picked up the phone and called their admissions office. It didn't make sense that they wouldn't want me as their student.

"You left out your social security number. We couldn't process your application, so we sent a blanket rejection letter," the admissions counselor explained.

"Oh. Is that a problem?" I asked.

"Well, without a social security number, we can't process your financial aid."

"So, if I don't have a social security number, I can't go to school?"

I wasn't sure if the counselor on the other end of the phone knew I was implying that I was undocumented, but the conversation made me feel like I was standing on shaky ground.

"No, I don't think that would matter," the woman said. "We could review your application again, but you'd be entirely on your own when it comes to paying tuition."

The tuition was around $30,000 a year. There was no way my parents or I could ever come up with that kind of money. As an undocumented student, I wasn't eligible for financial aid. I also couldn't apply for student loans, and my parents couldn't cosign a loan either, because they were not permanent residents or US citizens.

I realized that the form for every school I'd applied to included a box for a social security number—and that I'd left that spot blank on every single application. I had no choice. I didn't have a social security number. I could study more to get higher grades, I could be involved in extracurricular activities, but there was nothing I could do to get a social security number.

Would that mean I couldn't go to college?

I tried to push the thought out of my mind.

That blank box, the lack of those nine numbers, held me back.

I was feeling particularly down about it one day as I sat with my favorite teacher, Mr. G. He was my super-quirky pre-AP physics teacher. Everyone loved him, and I was definitely a teacher's pet. I had a free period at the end of the school day. Because I was a senior, I could have gone home early, but I didn't want to. Mr. G let me help him grade tests, or sometimes I just did my homework in his classroom.

"I don't know if I'm going to be able to go to college," I told him. I didn't explain everything, but I said that because of my parents' "situation," we couldn't apply for financial aid. I'm not sure if he understood what I meant, but it didn't seem to matter.

"Well, don't give up," he told me. "You should still apply to college. Just apply. Apply everywhere you can. See what happens. I'll keep writing you the best letters of recommendation, and they're going to *have* to let you in."

With his encouragement, I kept applying, even to schools like Harvard and Dartmouth. He insisted I had the grades and ambition to get in. I'll never forget when he wrote me a letter of recommendation for Dartmouth. He wouldn't let me read it, but he said, "If this letter of recommendation doesn't get you in, then the world is doomed."

He also encouraged me to apply to the University of Texas in Austin. I told him I wanted to go someplace far away, but he insisted, "It's a great school. It's one of the top schools in the country. Don't dismiss it." I agreed to follow his advice, but then I put off submitting the application. I just didn't feel like it was the right school for me.

My mom kept insisting we would find a way to pay for the best school that accepted me. I believed her. Her encouragement, optimism, and never-ending work ethic gave me hope. I submitted applications, and then waited, and hoped.

TRAGEDY

My DAD PICKED ME UP from school every day like clock-work during my senior year. So I was surprised to see Aris waiting in her car when I walked out of school one day in the middle of November. Aris had never picked me up at school before, *ever*.

"Hey," I said as I opened the passenger door. "What are you doing here?"

"Mom was in an accident."

"What?" I said, my heart sinking to my stomach. I could see that she had been crying.

"She was setting up at Fort Sam Houston and the fuel tank on the roasted corn machine exploded."

"Oh my God," I said, covering my face with my hands.

"It blew her right onto the sidewalk. It's a miracle she's not burned, but..." Aris turned away and started to cry.

"Oh my God, Aris, is she okay?" My mouth became completely dry.

"She's at the hospital," Aris said. "They don't know if she's going to wake up."

"Take me to see her now!"

Aris wiped the tears from her eyes and began driving. The next thing I remember is standing in a bright hallway with ugly white tile floors, staring at my mom in a hospital bed through a big window. She had a tube down her throat to help her breathe. There were wires all over her. Her beautiful hair was shaved off. She looked frail. She didn't look like my mother.

I wanted to cry, but the tears were stuck and wouldn't come out.

A doctor walked out of the room and started talking to my dad.

My dad looked at me and said, *"Dile que te diga a ti."*

"My dad doesn't speak English fluently. He said you can talk to me," I said to the doctor.

"Okay. She's lucky to be alive." My heart sank deeper.

"All we've been able to do at this point is try to contain the swelling. There's not much more we can do but wait and see how she responds. We have every reason to hold out hope, but I have to let you know there is a chance she won't make it," he said.

Finally the river of tears started flowing from my eyes.

I wasn't prepared to hear those words, or to translate them to my family. But there was no one else to do it.

My dad wiped his tears. My sister cried loudly, "No, no, no!"

"Aris, we have to be strong for Julio and Dad."

Julio was only seven years old. I didn't know how I was going to tell him. Phone calls were made. My aunt, Uncle Mike, and Nay boarded planes to San Antonio the very next morning. They all had tourist visas and could make the trip. Before they arrived, the phone rang at home.

I ran to the kitchen from my bedroom and picked up the call.

"Hello, is Mr. Arce there? This is the neurosurgeon from Brooke Army Medical Center," a man said in a serious tone.

"Hi, this is his daughter, Julissa. I'll need to translate for him," I said to the doctor. "Papa! It's the hospital!" I yelled.

The doctor told me they needed to do emergency surgery on my mom because her brain was swelling. They would need to cut out a piece of her brain, because the skull is a fixed space; it can't expand. The only way for my mom to survive was to cut out small pieces and hope the swelling stopped.

"What happens next?" I asked the doctor.

My dad was standing next to me, looking at me with sad eyes.

The doctor continued, "If that doesn't contain the swelling, we'll have to cut more pieces from her brain, and that would cause more damage."

I was trying to absorb all of this while translating it for my dad because they needed his permission to operate.

"You have to tell us now. We don't have much time," the doctor said.

I didn't even finish explaining it to my dad before I answered: "Yes. He says yes. Operate on my mom."

I made the decision by myself, and as I hung up the phone I realized that whatever happened next was because of me. I explained everything to my dad more slowly, and he agreed that I did the right thing.

It was a long surgery. Thankfully the accident happened on the military base, and a world-renowned neurosurgeon was assigned to my mom's case. We all felt lucky that he was operating on my mom, and we hoped that it was God's way of watching over her. My Christian upbringing and prayer played a role in my life when I was younger, but I had not prayed much since. I felt selfish praying when I didn't spend time in church anymore. But I prayed anyway.

When the doctor finally stepped out of the operating room, we were all sitting in the waiting area. My aunt had a rosary in her hand. Aris was resting her head on Nay's shoulder. My dad and I were sitting next to each other. The doctor walked up to me and said, "Your mom is very strong. She made it through the surgery."

"Thank God! When can we see her?" I asked.

Then he explained one of the hardest things I've ever heard in my life. The only way to keep her alive after the surgery was to put her in a coma.

"I do have to warn you that there is a very small chance she might not wake up," he said.

"You purposely put her in a coma?" I cried.

Everyone got up from their seats and came closer to me.

The doctor continued to explain that when my mom woke up from the coma, she might act like a child. She would need to relearn how to walk and talk, and she might not remember us. She would need a lot of care for a long time.

"Oh my God. How long will it be before she fully recovers?" I asked.

"It may be years before she's back to normal, if she's ever back to normal," the doctor explained.

His words felt like a giant door closing on my future.

I'm the one who's going to have to take care of my mom.

I'm not sure why I felt all the responsibility would fall on me. I have two older sisters, a dad, and a large extended family. But that was my first thought: *I'll have to take care of my mom forever.*

After the doctor left, I explained everything to my family. They were either stunned or crying and wiping their tears away.

With my mom by my side I felt I could do anything. I could solve any problem. Nothing was impossible for her, and therefore nothing was impossible for me either.

She was the one who assured me that we'd find a way to send me to college. How could I do that on my own now? How could I possibly earn a degree while also taking care of her? How was I supposed to figure anything out by myself without her?

I felt selfish. I was thinking of myself when all that mattered was for my mom to live. But I couldn't help it. I was a senior in high school. This was an important year for me. My entire future was at stake—a future that I could no longer even try to imagine. The next step was college, and even that seemed out of reach now.

A month passed, and I quit the dance team. I had to go work at our small jewelry shop after school every day now. I had responsibilities at the funnel cake stand every weekend too. We couldn't afford to stop working, especially with the hospital bills for my mother's care. Every night when I went to bed, I prayed, "Dear God, please let my mom wake up from the coma. I don't care if I have to take care of her forever; please just let her wake up. Please let this nightmare end. Amen."

A week before Christmas, my mom finally opened her eyes. I was so relieved to see her awake. I couldn't stop sobbing. But it didn't take long for reality to set in.

At the doctor's directions we asked her a series of questions.

"What's your name?"

"Luisa," she said in a voice that didn't sound like hers.

"How many kids do you have?"

"Three, three daughters," she said, and then she started crying. "Did the baby survive?" she asked.

"What baby?" Aris asked.

For days she kept asking if the baby survived. It finally occurred to us that she thought she was still pregnant with Julio. Her sense of time was completely gone.

The doctor insisted it wasn't permanent. "She'll get better over time." But all I could see was that my mom was completely *off*. Her beautiful hair had been shaved, and now she had little gray hairs growing back. She aged dramatically in a short period of time. It made me so sad. People used to confuse my mom and Aris for siblings before her accident. She no longer looked like Aris's sister.

My mom made remarkable progress those next few months. I shouldn't have been surprised. My mother is fierce. By the spring of 2001 she was walking and talking again. Someone who didn't know her might have thought she was back to normal. I think she felt that way at times too, because as soon as she started feeling better she wanted to go back to work. But she would get tired very quickly. Those of us who were close to her could see that she was still not back to her old self.

She would be okay one minute, and then she would say something that didn't make sense. She would ask me a question and I'd answer, and then five minutes later she'd ask me again. She was forgetful, and we didn't feel it was safe for her to work at the funnel cake stand.

Nay took a semester off from college in Mexico so she could stay in San Antonio and help out. She was still the same tough girl I remembered as a child. One day we took my mom to the mall so she could walk around. We came to an escalator, and she didn't want to get on it.

"Mom, just get on the escalator. Stop being like that!" Nay yelled.

"Stop it, Nay! She's scared of the escalator!" I yelled back at her. "There has to be an elevator somewhere. We'll meet you upstairs. Don't pressure her to get on the escalator."

I worried about how my mom would be treated if I ever moved away for college. Every time I tried to imagine it, I simply stopped thinking about it. I couldn't allow myself to dream that big, because when I actually took a step back and thought of the future, all I saw was uncertainty.

GRADUATION

"I DON'T THINK I AM going to college next year," I said to Tio Mike while he was driving me to school one morning. My uncle had been living with us since my mom's accident and sometimes would drop me off at school while my dad took my mom for her physical therapy.

Nay went back to Mexico after the holidays to start her last semester in college. My uncle became our lifeline. He even threw me a big eighteenth birthday party at Olive Garden and invited twenty of my friends. Because of him, I started smiling again.

"Keep applying to colleges. You've worked too hard. Your mother would want you to go," he said.

So that was what I did. I put long hours into getting As and applying to every college I could find. I frantically filled out dozens of applications for schools I had barely even heard of, in any faraway place that might take me away from everything, but the rejections kept coming, over and over and over again.

I kept applying anyway.

"So, did you send out all of your college applications?" Mr. G asked me when we were sitting in his classroom, grading papers.

"I think so," I said. "I applied pretty much everywhere."

"Including the University of Texas?" he asked me.

I looked down at the desk and didn't say anything.

"Julissa. It's a great school. It could be perfect for you. If there's still any time to get your application in, I really think you should apply."

"All right. A lot of schools are already past deadline, but I'll look into it."

That afternoon, I realized the deadline was the very next day. The next morning my uncle Mike drove me to Austin to drop off my application in person. I remember picking the business school as my first choice because it was ranked in the top five in the country, not because I wanted to major in business. I was still sure I didn't want to attend UT, but I didn't want to let Mr. G down. He'd done too much to help me.

My uncle parked the car and we walked together to the admissions office. The campus was huge and beautiful. Seeing all the college students walking around filled me with anticipation and hope. Maybe someone like me could go to college despite my immigration status.

But by the end of the school year, I'd received rejection letters from every college I'd applied to, except one: Hendrix College, a liberal arts school in a tiny town in Arkansas that I'd picked out of a book. But I couldn't afford the tuition.

I tried to stay positive. I kept moving forward as if going to college were a possibility. I had a phone call with the girl Hendrix selected to be my roommate. We talked about what we would bring to set up our dorm room. And the whole time, I knew that I wouldn't be able to go unless some lottery-sized miracle came along to give my family and me a whole new start.

I spoke with Mr. G, and he suggested that I enroll at the local community college, San Antonio College (SAC).

"Are you kidding me?" I said.

There was a phrase among college-bound students at Roosevelt High: "Those who can't hack it, SAC it." I had worked so hard to attend a four-year college where my grades mattered in the admissions process. Enrolling in a two-year school where anyone could attend seemed unfair. Ultimately, though, I couldn't even afford to SAC it. I was still without a social security number or financial aid, and the deadline for making a down payment on tuition at Hendrix came and went.

I walked across the stage at my graduation in a cap and gown and received my diploma with no idea if and when I would go to college. I graduated in the top 5 percent of my class. My whole family was proud of me. I had a huge smile. And yet all of us were worried. I thought I had everything going for me: I was a high school graduate and an honors student, and I had great friends, mentors, and a supportive family. And yet, I had no options.

I spent the weekend after graduation with powdered sugar in my hair, covered in a layer of fryolator grease, and sweating in the scorching Texas sun, with one thought on my mind.

Is this what my life is now?

I tried not to get down about it, and to take on my mother's attitude: *I'll find a way. I will.* But every time I tried to think about my future, it was like looking through a haze of powdered sugar. I couldn't see the life of wealth and happiness that I'd been working toward for so long. Somehow, when I wasn't looking, my American Dream crashed into a giant wall.

HOUSE BILL 1403

Uncle Mike handed me a piece of paper as soon as I walked into the house. The paper had a phone number on it, and a name: Rick Noriega.

"What is this?" I asked him.

"Julissa, you have to call the number. Right now, before the office closes. This could be it. This could be what we've been waiting for."

It was July. I was hot and tired after making funnel cakes all day. I looked at him with a blank stare.

"They passed a bill allowing undocumented students to go to college here in Texas," he said.

"What?" I said in disbelief.

San Antonio is a friendly city toward immigrants, but we still lived in a state where undocumented immigrants are often intimidated and treated poorly.

"It was on the news. That number is for the office of the state congressman who helped pass the bill. Call," he said.

I was stunned. I didn't know that this kind of bill was even being discussed. I didn't know what else to do except call the number. The operator put me through to Rick Noriega's office, and then I was on the phone with Linda Christofilis, Mr. Noriega's assistant. I asked her if I might be eligible to go to college under this new law my uncle had heard about.

"House Bill 1403, yes," she said. "Well, why don't you tell me a little bit about yourself, and we'll see if we can help."

I had learned never to speak to anyone about my immigration status, especially someone in a government position, but there was something about Linda's voice that made me feel safe. So I started talking. I told her about when I arrived in the United States, how I came to live here, and that I had just graduated high school in the top 5 percent of my class. She asked for all of my information, and I gave it to her: address, phone number, everything.

"Well," Linda said, "you're exactly the type of student this bill was written for."

"Really?" I said, my voice cracking. "I applied to UT and other schools. The applications were filled out, with recommendations and everything. But they rejected me because I don't have a social security number. I had my heart set on going to college this year. So is there any chance this bill is retroactive? Or will I have to wait until next year to apply to school again?"

There was silence for a moment.

"You know, that's a good question. Hold on a second," she said.

She put me on hold for what felt like forever.

"Hi," she said. "Yes, it is retroactive and could be applied to your applications to schools for this current year."

"That's amazing!" I said. "What do I need to do? How can I make this happen?"

"Where else did you apply in the state of Texas?" she asked.

"Only UT Austin."

Linda told me they would type up a letter for the

congressman to sign and send it to the UT admissions office to reevaluate my application.

"Really?" My smile got so big I thought my cheeks would break.

"Yes, and if your grades are what you say they are and everything else is in order, I think you'll have a very good shot at getting in—*and* you'll qualify for the Texas Grant. It's for five thousand dollars, so it'll cover a significant portion of your in-state tuition. You'll have to keep your grades up if you want to hold on to that grant once you get it," she said.

"Oh my God. That's fantastic. I will work hard, I promise."

I was ecstatic that my grades finally mattered.

"Well, good. The congressman will be excited to hear about your case, and I'm just so glad you called today."

She was glad that I called that day!

"I don't even know what to say," I said. "Thank you so much!"

"Thank you, Julissa. I hope this all works out for you. We'll be in touch soon."

My parents, my brother, and Uncle Mike were all

gathered around expectantly, waiting for me to get off the phone.

I covered my face with my hands and cried a little. I looked up and said, "The bill applies to me, and the congressman is going to send a letter to UT asking them to reevaluate my application."

Then we all cried.

My mother kept saying, "I knew we would find a way."

House Bill 1403 was better than winning the lottery. The chance of a law being passed at the exact moment I needed it was proof God existed and He loved me.

Texas was the first state in the United States to allow undocumented students to attend public universities, pay in-state tuition, and receive state financial aid. Since that day, only twenty states have passed similar laws. But in Georgia, South Carolina, and Alabama, there are laws to ban undocumented students from pursuing a higher education.

I was overwhelmed with joy, but I also had some lingering fears. Perhaps UT was fully enrolled and wouldn't have room for any more students. Maybe I'd have to wait a year to apply again. But at that moment I could finally breathe a little. I started seeing a future again.

Every day I would run out from my house to the mail-box and sort through everything, looking for a letter from UT. Finally, a couple of weeks after that phone call with Linda, I recognized the UT logo in the upper-left-hand corner of an envelope. I didn't even wait to get back inside. I tore open the envelope. Standing right there on the street, I felt tears streaming down my face.

I can't believe this is really happening.

I ran inside and yelled, "I got accepted to UT. I got in!"

My mom and dad hugged me, and each other. My uncle told me something I will never forget: "Congratulations. But remember that you earned it. Nobody gave you this."

He taught me to recognize that in life you need two things to be successful: preparation and opportunities. My mom, my dad, and the rest of my entire family helped me to be prepared, and now the state of Texas was giving me the opportunity I needed.

"This is just the beginning," he said. "This is just the first step."

SAYING GOOD-BYE

MY MOTHER WAS STILL NOT well. One morning while we were driving her to physical therapy, she suffered what we learned was a seizure. We were making a left turn when my mom started shaking uncontrollably in the front seat. Her mouth moved completely to the left and she started drooling.

"Tio, drive fast, there is an emergency clinic up ahead."

I ran into the front office and yelled, "Help! My mom is in shock." I tried to describe what was happening to her.

"Please help us!" I screamed.

Finally two men with a stretcher took my mom inside. The doctor told us my mom had suffered a seizure. She would need to take medicine to help her avoid them in the future.

I began to worry again that I would have to stay in San Antonio to take care of my mom. But luckily, it didn't take long for her to recover.

A couple of weeks later we visited Austin to find student housing. There was no more housing available on campus, but we managed to find an off-campus dorm a couple of blocks away from the UT campus. We put a small deposit down, but as we drove away, it became clear to all of us that the rent was going to be more than my family could afford on top of all our monthly expenses.

"We'll find a way," my mom insisted.

A few days after we came back from Austin, my uncle sat us all down and said he'd made a decision.

"Your mom and Julio are going to live in Taxco."

I could see that looking after my mom was taking a toll on my uncle. He'd left everything behind in Mexico to help us. My mom would have Mama Silvia and the rest of the family to help her. San Antonio was close enough to Austin that I could make the trip every weekend to work the funnel cake stand to help pay for my college expenses.

My dad's feelings weren't taken into consideration, but my mom agreed it was for the best. My dad would stay behind to tie up any loose ends, and then join them in Taxco. It happened so quickly I could barely wrap my mind around it.

In no time at all, I was packing up my things and moving into a dorm. I went from a crowded house full of family to a crowded dormitory full of strangers. Just like that, I was shaking hands with a new roommate, introducing myself to our neighbors—and saying good-bye to my parents and Julio as they headed back to San Antonio without me. I was excited and nervous about what the future would bring. Every other student I saw around campus seemed thrilled to be away from home, but I kept wondering when I would see my parents and brother again.

There weren't any new laws that offered me a chance to gain US citizenship. There was nothing I could do to change my immigration status. My only choice was to continue pursuing my dreams or give up. I could have passed on the grant and moved back to Mexico with my

214

parents. Perhaps I would be able to come back to the United States in the future. But I knew that as soon as I crossed the border, I would instantly be banned from the United States for ten years—that's still the current law. *Ten years.* I couldn't wait that long to go to college. I had worked too hard, and my parents had sacrificed too much. America was my home.

By the time I started at UT, the desire to help my parents had turned into something more for me. It was a fire burning deep inside—a drive to fix all the things that were wrong. My parents never asked me to take care of them. But in my family, there's simply an unwritten rule that we help one another out. It's a big part of my Mexican culture.

My parents always told me: "School is your salvation. Education is your salvation. Education is your way out." Now, with a chance to go to one of the best business schools in the country, I set my sights high from the very start. I decided I wanted to be a powerful businesswoman, and travel the world. I wanted to buy a mechanic shop for my dad and a jewelry store for my mom, and take them on vacations. I didn't want my little brother to have the same worries as me. *That* became my American Dream: to help my family.

I needed to believe deep in my soul that someone like me could make it in America, especially on the emotional day when I took my mom, Julio, and Uncle Mike to the airport. There were people everywhere trying to get cabs, heading to their gates, or saying good-bye to their families. We were running late and it was happening too fast.

"I love you," I said to Julio as I held his little face in my hands. "Behave, okay? Be good with Mom."

"I will," he said.

I hugged my mom for a long time. I don't remember what we said to each other. I'm not sure we said anything. I just remember that I soaked the shoulder of her shirt with my tears—and she soaked my shoulder too.

"Mama Silvia and I will take good care of her," Uncle Mike said. "I promise."

"I know you will. I know."

I watched them walk onto the ramp until they disappeared around the corner and onto the plane, not knowing when I would see them again.

From the outside, my freshman year in college looked like any other. Madison House, my dorm, was small, so everyone got to know one another very well. We bonded over our love for taquitos (mouth-watering, deep-fried corn tortillas stuffed with cheese, served on Wednesdays), movie nights, and other dorm-wide activities. It was the normal stuff that any college student might expect.

There were also many things that I didn't have to worry about anymore. My dad wasn't screaming at me. I didn't have to take care of my mom or help my little brother with his homework. It was so good to just be me, to be selfish, to only worry about myself. To be normal. But once Friday came around, I was reminded how *not* normal I was. While everyone started on their weekend plans, I boarded a bus for the ninety-minute ride back to San Antonio to sell funnel cakes. I was instantly reminded of how much my mom, my brother, and my father were giving up just so that I could go to college. How could I not feel like I owed them everything?

I saw my dad briefly over the first few weekends. I was

thankful to have him there to help me set up the funnel cake stand at the outdoor market. I was happy to still have him in San Antonio. But I didn't live with him during those weekends. I stayed with Aris and her husband. I felt guilty about staying with her instead of at home with my dad. He was sad about it too, but I wouldn't give in. He hadn't quit drinking alcohol yet, so I left him alone in our old home.

A month later my dad finished selling most of our possessions and bought a bus ticket to Mexico. Aris and I drove him to the bus station one Saturday night after we closed the funnel cake stand.

"I love you, *mija*," he said, and boarded the bus. He kept his eyes on me until the bus turned the corner out of the station.

When I couldn't see my dad anymore, all the tears began to roll down my face. My parents and I had switched places. They were now in Mexico while I stayed in America. But I didn't know when I would be able to visit them. My family would be gone. That was the true price of my college education.

The next night I took a bus from the same station back to school. On Monday morning I went to my chemistry class in an auditorium with four hundred students. I got back my first college exam. I got an A. I wiped my tears away.

When class let out, I walked to the six-pack, a lawn in the middle of campus. It was packed with students throwing footballs around, doing homework, and eating lunch. I lay on the grass, feeling the Texas sun on my face. I took out my test from my backpack and looked at it again.

I made it.

I almost didn't survive all the challenges I had faced at home, at school, and with my immigration status, but I had been really strong and fought for my dreams. Here I was, a student at one of the best universities in the country. My mom had been right all along. Someone like me could make it in America.

THE YEARS SINCE

In May 2005, I graduated with honors from the University of Texas at Austin with a bachelor of business administration in finance. My mom, Tio Mike, Aris, and Nay came to my graduation ceremony. Tiffani also attended my commencement, and we continue to be great friends to this day. My dad's visa had expired by then, and he couldn't make the trip to Austin.

Throughout college, I waited and prayed for the immigration laws to change. I hoped there might be some sort of process, a line I could get in, or a fine I could pay to fix my immigration status, but there was nothing. I didn't qualify for anything. So when I was nineteen, I did the only thing I felt like I could do to go on living my life: I bought a fake green card and a social security card.

After college, I moved to New York City to work at Goldman Sachs on Wall Street, one of the most prestigious financial institutions in the world. I lived in constant fear of anyone finding out that my documents were fake and I wasn't supposed to be working. But despite the challenges and fears, I became a vice president at the age of twenty-seven. I had achieved all my professional goals.

One night in 2007, I called my dad in Mexico, and we had a long heart-to-heart conversation. I asked for his forgiveness for calling the cops. He asked me to forgive him for his drinking, for hitting me, and for putting me in a position where I had to call the police. I am so grateful for that conversation with my dad. In September 2007, Nay called me at work and told me our dad was very sick. I debated for hours over whether I should go to Mexico. If I left the United States, I wouldn't be able to come back. In the middle of my agonizing over what I should do, my dad passed away, and I never got to see him alive again.

A year later, I got married to my college boyfriend, and because he is an American citizen, I was finally able to fix my immigration status. In August 2014, I became an American citizen, twenty years after I first came to live in the United States. My first trip out of the country was to Mexico. It was a very emotional trip. I was finally back in the country of my birth. Mama Silvia had also passed away, and she and my dad are buried in the same place. I visited their graves and gave them thanks for all the sacrifices they made for me.

As for Julio, he came to live with me in New York City shortly after our dad passed away. In May 2007, he graduated from Texas Tech University with a degree in economics and started his first job. I am very proud of him. Aris has been married for eighteen years and has four boys! Nay still lives in Mexico, is married, and has a daughter and a son.

I see my mom at least twice a year, when I travel to Mexico or take her on vacations. For her sixtieth birthday, I took her on a weeklong trip to Costa Rica.

I left Wall Street in 2014 and since then I have worked to advance the rights of undocumented immigrants. I cofounded the Ascend Educational Fund, a college mentorship and scholarship program for immigrant students in New York City, regardless of their immigration status. Education changed my life; it opened doors of opportunity, and now it is my turn to open doors for others.

ACKNOWLEDGMENTS

To my mom and dad, who sacrificed everything for me, thank you.

This book is not just mine; so many people made it possible. I have to thank my sisters, Aris and Nay, and my brother, Julio, who have supported me and loved me throughout my journey.

Someone Like Me would not be what it is without the guidance and support of Reyna Grande. Her writing has inspired me, and her mentorship has made me dig deep to become a better and more vulnerable writer.

Someone Like Me belongs to my friends, to my teachers (thank you, Mr. G; I would not be here without you), to my mentors, and to the thousands of people who fought for my right to go to college and who worked tirelessly to pass the Texas Dream Act in 2001.

I cannot thank my literary agent, Lisa Leshne, enough. She has believed in me from the very first coffee we shared in New York City. Her friendship and support have been invaluable in my journey as a writer.

My editor, Nikki Garcia, believed in this book so passionately that she went above and beyond the normal duties and worked tirelessly to bring out the best in me as a writer. I am so grateful for Michelle Campbell, Stefanie Hoffman, Sasha Illingworth, Farrin Jacobs, Katharine Mc-Anarney, Elizabeth Rosenbaum, Victoria Stapleton, Angela Taldone, Megan Tingley, and the rest of the team at Little, Brown Books for Young Readers for believing in my dream to bring my story to young audiences. Before my story became a book for young readers, Kate Hartson at Center Street took a chance on me and published my first book, *My (Underground) American Dream*. I will be forever grateful.

My deepest gratitude to my husband, Fernando, who is my biggest supporter and makes this dream possible with his patience and love.

Finally, thank you to the millions of immigrants who have come before me, risked their lives, lost their lives, and left their families and land behind to come to America. Thank you. Because without you, America would not exist.